247 Most Popular Excel Tips : From Beginner to 1

Copyright © 2023 par David Lefek

All rights reserved. No part of this book may be reproduced or transmitted in any form or by any means, electronic or mechanical, including photocopying, recording or by any information storage and retrieval system, without permission in writing from the author.

Disclaimer: The tips and techniques in this book are provided "as is" without warranty of any kind, either express or implied, including but not limited to the implied warranties of merchantability and fitness for a particular purpose. The author and publisher shall have neither liability nor responsibility to any person or entity with respect to any loss or damages arising from the information contained in this book.

Trademark Acknowledgments: All trademarks mentioned in this book are the property of their respective owners. The use of trademarks in this book is solely for educational purposes, and does not imply endorsement or affiliation with the respective trademark owners.

ISBN : 9798386874087
First edition, 2023

Contents

3D Reference in Excel 12
Absolute Reference (Excel Shortcut) 14
Activate a Sheet using VBA 16
Add a Button in Excel 18
Add a Column in Excel 20
Add a Horizontal Line in a Chart in Excel 22
Add a Vertical Line in a Chart in Excel 24
Add and Delete a Worksheet in Excel 26
Add and Remove Hyperlinks in Excel 28
Add Barcode 30
Add Calculated Field and Item (Formulas in a Pivot Table) 31
Add Column (Excel Shortcut) 33
Add Hours to Time in Excel 34
Add Indent (Excel Shortcut) 35
Add Leading Zeros in Excel 37
Add Minutes to Time in Excel 38
Add Month to a Date in Excel 39
Add New Line in a Cell in Excel (Line Break) 40
Add New Sheet (Excel Shortcut) 41
Add or Remove Grand Total in a Pivot Table in Excel 42
Add Ranks in Pivot Table in Excel 43
Add Running Total in a Pivot Table in Excel 45
Add Secondary Axis in Excel Charts 46
Add Serial Numbers 47
Add Watermark in Excel 49
Add Years to Date in Excel 51
Add-Subtract Week from a Date in Excel 52

Align Center (Excel Shortcut) 53

Apply Accounting Number Format in Excel 54

Apply and Remove Filter (Excel Shortcut) 55

Apply and Remove Filter (Excel Shortcut) 56

Apply Border (Excel Shortcut) 57

Apply Comma Style in Excel 59

Apply Conditional Formatting to a Pivot Table 60

Apply Date Format (Excel Shortcut) 62

Apply Multiple Filters to Columns 63

Apply Print Titles in Excel (Set Row 1 to Print on Every Page) 64

Apply Time Format (Excel Shortcut) 66

Auto Fit (Excel Shortcut) 68

AutoFormat 70

AutoSum (Excel Shortcut) 71

Average TOP 5 Values in Excel 72

Bullet Points 73

Calculate Compound Interest in Excel 74

Calculate Cube Root in Excel 75

Calculate Percentage Variance (Difference) in Excel 77

Calculate Simple Interest in Excel 78

Calculate the Age 79

Calculate the Coefficient of Variation (CV) in Excel 80

Calculate the Ratio 81

Calculate the Weighted Average in Excel 82

Calculate Time Difference Between Two Times in Excel 84

Capitalize First Letter in Excel 85

Cell Message 86

Cell Style (Title, Calculation, Total, Headings…) in Excel 87

Center a Worksheet Horizontally and Vertically in Excel 89

Change Column to Row (Vice Versa) in Excel 91

Change Date Format in Excel 92

Change Time Format in Excel 93

Chart Formatting 94

Chart Template 96

Check IF 0 (Zero) Then Blank in Excel 98

Check IF a Value Exists in a Range in Excel 99

Check Mark (Excel Shortcut) 101

Clear Contents (Excel Shortcut) 102

Clear Formatting 103

Clipboard 104

Close (Excel Shortcut) 106

Combine IF and AND Functions in Excel 107

Combine IF and OR Functions in Excel 108

Compare Two Cells in Excel 109

Compare Two Dates in Excel 111

Concatenate with a Line Break in Excel 113

Conditional Ranking in Excel using SUMPRODUCT Function [RANKIF] 114

Convert Date to Number in Excel 115

Count Between Two Numbers (COUNTIFS) in Excel 116

Count Blank (Empty) Cells using COUNTIF in Excel 118

Count Cells Less than a Particular Value (COUNTIF) in Excel 119

Count Cells Not Equal To in Excel (COUNTIF) 120

Count Cells That Are Not Blank in Excel 121

Count Cells with Text in Excel 122

Count Greater Than 0 (COUNTIF) in Excel 123

4

Count Specific Characters in Excel 124
Count the Total Number of Cells from a Range in Excel 125
Count Unique Values in a Pivot Table in Excel 126
COUNT Vs. COUNTA 127
Count Words 129
Count Years Between Two Dates in Excel 131
Create a Bullet Chart in Excel 132
Create a Data Validation with Date Range 134
Create a Dynamic Chart Range in Excel 136
Create a HEAT MAP in Excel (Simple Steps) + Template 137
Create a HISTOGRAM in Excel 138
Create a Horizontal Filter in Excel 140
Create a Milestone Chart in Excel 141
Create a Pivot Table from Multiple Worksheets 143
Create a Population Pyramid Chart in Excel 144
Create a Star Rating Template in Excel 146
Create a Step Chart in Excel 147
Create a Tornado Chart in Excel 149
Create a Yes – No Drop Down in Excel 151
Create Interactive Charts in Excel 153
Create Pivot Chart in Excel 155
Create WAFFLE CHART in Excel 157
Currency Format (Excel Shortcut) 159
Custom Date Formats in Excel 160
Days in a Month 162
Default Chart 164
Delete (Excel Shortcut) 166
Delete a Pivot Table in Excel 167

Delete Blank Rows in Excel 168
Delete Cell (Excel Shortcut) 169
Delete Hidden Rows in Excel 170
Delete Row(s) (Excel Shortcut) 171
Delete Sheet (Excel Shortcut) 172
Deselect Cells in Excel 173
Display Units 174
Does Not Equal Operator in Excel 175
Draw a Line in Excel 176
Edit Cell (Excel Shortcut) 178
Excel Funnel Chart (Template + Steps to Create) 179
Excel Funnel Chart (Template + Steps to Create) 180
Excel Gantt Chart Template 182
Fill Color (Excel Shortcut) 184
Fill Handle in Excel 186
Filter a Pivot Table in Excel 187
Find and Replace in Excel 189
Font Color with Custom Formatting 190
Format Painter 192
Formula Bar in Excel 193
Formulas in Conditional Formatting 194
Freeze Pane (Excel Shortcut) 196
Full Screen (Excel Shortcut) 198
Get Day Name from a Date in Excel 199
Get Day Number of Year in Excel 200
Get First Day of the Month in Excel (Beginning of the Month) 201
Get Quarter from a Date [Fiscal + Calendar] in Excel 202
Get Sheet Name in Excel 204

Get the File Name in Excel 205

Get Years of Service in Excel 206

Group (Excel Shortcut) 208

Group Dates in a Pivot Table 209

Group Worksheets in the Excel 211

Hidden Cells 213

Hide and Unhide a Workbook in Excel 215

Hide Axis Labels 217

Hide Formula in Excel 218

Hide Gap 219

Highlight Blank Cells 220

Highlight Dates Between Two Dates in Excel 221

Hyperlink (Excel Shortcut) 222

IF Cell is Blank (Empty) using IF + ISBLANK in Excel 223

IF Negative Then Zero (0) in Excel 224

IFERROR with VLOOKUP in Excel to Replace #N/A in Excel 225

Increase and Decrease Indent in Excel 227

Insert a People Graph in Excel 229

Insert an Arrow in a Cell in Excel 231

Insert Cell (Excel Shortcut) 232

Insert Current Date and Time 233

Link a Single Slicer with Multiple Pivot Tables 234

Lock Cells (Excel Shortcut) 236

Make a Copy of the Excel Workbook (File) 238

Make a Paragraph in a Cell in Excel 239

Make Negative Numbers Red in Excel 240

MAX IF in Excel 242

Merge – Unmerge Cells in Excel 244

Merge [Combine] Multiple Excel FILES into ONE WORKBOOK..245
Merge Cells in Excel without Losing Data in Excel 247
Merge-Unmerge Cells (Excel Shortcut) 248
Military Time (Get and Subtract) in Excel 250
Month Name 252
Month's Last Date 253
Move a Pivot Table 254
Move Data 255
Number of Months Between Two Dates in Excel 257
Open Go To Option (Excel Shortcut) 258
OR Logic in COUNTIF/COUNIFS in Excel 259
Paste Values (Excel Shortcut) 261
Percentage Format (Excel Shortcut) 262
Perform Two Way Lookup in Excel 264
Perform VLOOKUP in Power Query in Excel 265
Pictograph in Excel 267
Pivot Table Formatting 269
Pivot Table Keyboard Shortcuts 271
Pivot Table Timeline in Excel 273
Pivot Table using Multiple Files in Excel 274
Print a Graph Paper in Excel (Square Grid Template) 276
Print Titles 278
Quickly Concatenate Two Dates in Excel 280
R1C1 Reference Style in Excel 281
Random Numbers 283
1. **Randomize a List (Random Sort) in Excel** 283
Recover Unsaved Excel Files When Excel Crashed 286
Refresh a Pivot Table 287

Refresh All Pivot Tables at Once in Excel 288

Remove Drop Down List (Data validation) in Excel 289

Remove Pagebreak in Excel 290

Reverse VLOOKUP 291

Root of Number 292

Rotate Text in Excel (Text Orientation) 293

Round a Number to Nearest 1000, 100, and 10 in Excel 294

Round to Nearest .5, 5. 50 (Down-Up) in Excel 296

Row Vs Column in Excel (Difference) 297

Save Excel File (Workbook) as CSV (XLSX TO CSV) 298

Select Non-Continues Cells 299

Select Row (Excel Shortcut) 301

Sentence Case 302

Separate Date and Time in Excel 303

Separate names in Excel – (First & Last Name) 305

Shortcut for Unhide Columns (Excel Shortcut) 307

Show Formulas (Excel Shortcut) 308

Show Ruler in Excel 309

Smooth Line 310

Sort a Pivot Table in Excel 311

Sort Buttons 312

Sort By Date, Date, and Time & Reverse Date Sort in Excel 313

SPEEDOMETER Chart in Excel 316

Spell Check in Excel 318

Square a Number in Excel 320

Status Bar 321

Strikethrough 322

Subscript (Excel Shortcut) 323

Sum an Entire Column or a Row in Excel...324
Sum Greater Than Values using SUMIF..326
Sum Not Equal Values (SUMIFS) in Excel..328
Sum Only Visible Cells in Excel..329
Sum Random Cells in Excel...330
SUMIF / SUMIFS with an OR Logic in Excel.......................................331
SUMIF with Wildcard Characters in Excel..332
SUMIFS Date Range (Sum Values Between Two Dates Array).........334
SUMPRODUCT IF..335
SUMPRODUCT IF to Create a Conditional Formula in Excel..........336
Superscript (Excel Shortcut)...337
Switch Tabs (Excel Shortcut)..338
Theme Color..339
Thermometer Chart in Excel..341
Transpose (Excel Shortcut)...343
Undo-Redo...344
View Two Sheets Side by Side in Excel..346
VLOOKUP MATCH Combination in Excel...347
VLOOKUP with Multiple Criteria in Excel..349
Wildcard Characters in Excel...351
Wildcards with VLOOKUP in Excel..353
Worksheet Copy..355
Write (Type) Vertically in Excel..356
Years Between Dates in Excel..357
Zoom-In (Excel Shortcut)...358

Master Excel with 247 Popular Tips: From Beginner to Expert

Are you tired of wasting hours on tedious Excel tasks that could be done in minutes? Are you struggling to keep up with the latest features and shortcuts in Excel? Look no further than "247 Most Popular Excel Tips From Beginner to Expert"!

Excel is a powerful tool used by millions of people worldwide to organize data, create charts, and perform complex calculations. However, many users are unaware of the shortcuts and tricks that can save them time and effort. This book is designed to help both beginners and experts get the most out of Excel by providing a comprehensive collection of the most popular tips and techniques.

The book is organized into sections based on the level of expertise, from beginner to expert. Each section contains tips and techniques that are easy to understand and follow, with step-by-step instructions and screenshots to guide you through the process. Whether you are a beginner looking to learn the basics of Excel, or an expert seeking advanced techniques to take your skills to the next level, this book has something for everyone.

With "247 Most Popular Excel Tips From Beginner to Expert," you will learn how to streamline your workflow, save time, and become a more efficient Excel user. Whether you are a student, business professional, or simply someone who wants to improve their Excel skills, this book is an essential resource for anyone who wants to master Excel.

3D Reference in Excel

A 3D reference in Excel allows you to reference the same cell or range of cells on multiple worksheets in a workbook. This is useful when you want to perform a calculation or analysis on data that is spread across multiple worksheets.

Step-by-Step Guide:

- Open the Excel workbook that contains the worksheets you want to reference.
- In a blank cell, type an equal sign (=) to begin the formula.
- Click on the first worksheet tab that contains the data you want to reference.
- Select the cell or range of cells you want to reference.
- Type a comma (,) to separate the worksheet and cell/range references.
- Click on the next worksheet tab that contains the data you want to reference.
- Select the cell or range of cells you want to reference on this worksheet.
- Repeat steps 5-7 for each worksheet that contains data you want to reference.
- Complete the formula as desired, including any necessary operators and functions.
- Press Enter to calculate the result.

When using 3D references, be sure to include the sheet names in the reference. For example, if you want to reference cell A1 on the Sheet1, Sheet2, and Sheet3 worksheets, your formula should look like this: =SUM(Sheet1!A1, Sheet2!A1, Sheet3!A1)

Additional Tips:

- You can also use 3D references in functions that require a range argument, such as SUM and AVERAGE.
- You can use 3D references to create a dynamic summary worksheet that consolidates data from multiple worksheets.

Absolute Reference (Excel Shortcut)

An absolute reference in Excel is a reference to a specific cell that remains constant when copied or filled to other cells. This is useful when you want to reference a cell or range of cells in a formula that should not change as the formula is copied to other cells.

Step-by-Step Guide:

- Open the Excel workbook and navigate to the worksheet where you want to use an absolute reference.
- Select the cell where you want to enter the formula that will include an absolute reference.
- Type the formula and include a cell reference that you want to make absolute. For example, if you want to reference cell B2, type "=B2".
- Place your cursor on the cell reference in the formula and press the F4 key. This will add the dollar sign symbol ($) to the cell reference to make it an absolute reference. The dollar sign symbol should appear in front of both the column letter and row number, like this: "=$B$2".
- Press Enter to calculate the formula result.

Additional Tips:

- You can also use the F4 key to toggle between different types of references. For example, if you have a mixed reference (e.g. "$B2"), pressing F4 will cycle through "$B$2", "B$2", and "$B2" references.

- You can use absolute references in any formula that references cells, including arithmetic formulas, logical formulas, and lookup formulas.

Absolute references are especially useful when creating complex formulas or when copying formulas to multiple cells. By making certain cell references absolute, you can ensure that the formula always references the correct cells, regardless of where it is copied or filled.

Activate a Sheet using VBA

VBA (Visual Basic for Applications) is a programming language that you can use to automate tasks in Excel. One common task is to activate a specific worksheet in an Excel workbook. Activating a sheet means that it becomes the active sheet in the workbook, which allows you to interact with its contents.

Step-by-Step Guide:

- Open the Excel workbook and navigate to the VBA Editor by pressing Alt + F11 on your keyboard.
- In the VBA Editor, locate the Project Explorer window on the left-hand side of the screen. If the Project Explorer window is not visible, press Ctrl + R to display it.
- In the Project Explorer window, locate the workbook that contains the sheet you want to activate.
- Expand the workbook by clicking on the plus sign (+) next to its name.
- Expand the Sheets folder to view a list of all sheets in the workbook.
- Double-click on the sheet you want to activate. This will open the code window for that sheet.
- In the code window, type the following code: Sheets("SheetName").Activate
- Replace "SheetName" with the name of the sheet you want to activate. For example, if you want to activate a sheet called "Data", your code should look like this: Sheets("Data").Activate
- Save the changes to the VBA code by clicking on the Save button or pressing Ctrl + S on your keyboard.

- Close the VBA Editor window.
- Test the code by running it. To run the code, switch back to the Excel workbook and press Alt + F8 on your keyboard to open the Macros window. Select the macro you just created and click on the Run button.

Additional Tips:

- You can also use the worksheet's index number instead of its name to activate it. For example, if the sheet you want to activate is the third sheet in the workbook, you can use the following code: Sheets(3).Activate
- Activating a sheet is not always necessary, as you can reference cells on any sheet in the workbook without activating it. However, there may be situations where activating a sheet is useful, such as when you want to select a specific range or apply formatting to a range of cells on a specific sheet.

Add a Button in Excel

Adding a button in Excel allows you to quickly access a macro or a series of actions you have recorded in the Visual Basic Editor. This can save you time and make your Excel spreadsheets more efficient.

Step-by-Step Guide:

- Open the Excel workbook and click on the Developer tab in the Ribbon. If you don't see the Developer tab, right-click on any tab and select Customize the Ribbon. In the Excel Options dialog box, select the Developer checkbox and click on OK.
- In the Developer tab, click on the Insert button in the Controls group and select the Button control under Form Controls.
- Click and drag to draw the button on the worksheet.
- In the Assign Macro dialog box that appears, click on the New button to create a new macro or select an existing one from the list.
- In the Visual Basic Editor, write the code for the macro you want to run when the button is clicked.
- Close the Visual Basic Editor and save your macro.
- Right-click on the button and select Edit Text to change the text displayed on the button. You can also format the button by right-clicking on it and selecting Format Control.
- Test the button by clicking on it. The macro associated with the button will run.

Additional Tips:

- You can move the button to a different location on the worksheet by clicking and dragging it.
- You can also assign a keyboard shortcut to the button by right-clicking on it and selecting Assign Macro. In the Assign Macro dialog box, click on the Options button and select a keyboard shortcut from the list.
- You can use the button to run a variety of actions, such as formatting cells, sorting data, or importing data from an external source.

Add a Column in Excel

Adding a column in Excel allows you to insert a new column into your worksheet to store additional data or formulas. This can help you organize your data better and make your spreadsheets more useful.

Step-by-Step Guide:

- Select the column to the right of where you want to insert the new column. If you want to add a column to the beginning of the worksheet, select the entire first column by clicking on the column letter (A).
- Right-click on the selected column and choose Insert from the context menu. Alternatively, you can click on the Insert button in the Cells group on the Home tab and select Insert Sheet Columns.
- Excel will insert a new column to the left of the selected column.
- To rename the new column, click on the column header and type the new name. Alternatively, you can select the column header and use the F2 key to enter edit mode.
- Enter data or formulas into the new column as needed.

Additional Tips:

- If you have data in the column to the right of the inserted column, Excel will shift the data to the right to make room for the new column.
- You can also insert multiple columns at once by selecting the number of columns you want to

insert before right-clicking and selecting Insert or using the Insert Sheet Columns button.
- To delete a column, select the column and either right-click and choose Delete or use the Delete Sheet Columns button in the Cells group on the Home tab.

Add a Horizontal Line in a Chart in Excel

Adding a horizontal line in a chart in Excel can be useful for highlighting a specific value or threshold in your data. For example, you might want to add a horizontal line to show the average value of your data or to highlight a target value.

Step-by-Step Guide:

- Select the chart that you want to add a horizontal line to.
- Choose the data series to which you want to add the horizontal line, and then select the data point where you want the line to begin.
- Right-click on the data point and choose Add Trendline from the context menu.
- In the Format Trendline pane that appears on the right-hand side of the screen, select the Trendline Options tab.
- Under Trendline Options, choose the Linear trendline type and uncheck the boxes for Display Equation on Chart and Display R-Squared Value on Chart.
- Under Forecast, set the Forward and Backward values to 0.
- Under Line, select the Solid line type, and choose the desired color and width for the line.
- Under Axis, choose the Horizontal Axis option, and set the Axis Value to the value where you want the line to appear.
- Click the Close button to apply the trendline and horizontal line to the chart.

Additional Tips:

- If you want to add multiple horizontal lines to a chart, repeat the above steps for each line.
- You can adjust the properties of the horizontal line by selecting it and choosing the desired formatting options from the Format pane.
- If you want to remove a horizontal line, select it and press the Delete key.

Add a Vertical Line in a Chart in Excel

What does "Add a Vertical Line in a Chart in Excel" mean? Adding a vertical line in a chart in Excel can be useful for highlighting a specific date or point in time in your data. For example, you might want to add a vertical line to show the date when a new policy was implemented, or to highlight the point in time when a specific event occurred.

Step-by-Step Guide:

- Select the chart that you want to add a vertical line to.
- Choose the data series to which you want to add the vertical line, and then select the data point where you want the line to begin.
- Right-click on the data point and choose Add Trendline from the context menu.
- In the Format Trendline pane that appears on the right-hand side of the screen, select the Trendline Options tab.
- Under Trendline Options, choose the Linear trendline type and uncheck the boxes for Display Equation on Chart and Display R-Squared Value on Chart.
- Under Forecast, set the Forward and Backward values to 0.
- Under Line, select the Solid line type, and choose the desired color and width for the line.
- Under Axis, choose the Vertical Axis option, and set the Axis Value to the value where you want the line to appear.
- Click the Close button to apply the trendline and vertical line to the chart.

Additional Tips:

- If you want to add multiple vertical lines to a chart, repeat the above steps for each line.
- You can adjust the properties of the vertical line by selecting it and choosing the desired formatting options from the Format pane.
- If you want to remove a vertical line, select it and press the Delete key.

Add and Delete a Worksheet in Excel

Adding and deleting worksheets in Excel is a useful feature that allows you to manage and organize your data more effectively. Adding a new worksheet lets you work on a different set of data without affecting the current worksheet, while deleting a worksheet removes unnecessary data and declutters your workbook.

Step-by-Step Guide:

- Open your Excel workbook.
- Right-click on any existing worksheet tab at the bottom of the screen.
- From the context menu, select "Insert" to open the "Insert" dialog box.
- Select "Worksheet" and click the "OK" button.
- A new worksheet will be added to the workbook and will be given a default name (e.g. "Sheet1").
- To rename the worksheet, simply double-click on the tab and enter a new name.

How to Delete a Worksheet in Excel:

- Open your Excel workbook.
- Right-click on the worksheet tab you want to delete.
- From the context menu, select "Delete" to open the "Delete" dialog box.
- Select "Delete" again to confirm that you want to delete the worksheet.
- The worksheet will be removed from the workbook.

Additional Tips:

- You can also add a worksheet by clicking on the "+" icon to the right of the worksheet tabs.
- You can move worksheets within the workbook by clicking and dragging the worksheet tab to the desired position.
- Be careful when deleting worksheets, as it permanently removes all data on the worksheet and cannot be undone.

Add and Remove Hyperlinks in Excel

Adding hyperlinks in Excel is a useful feature that allows you to link to external sources, websites, or other parts of the same workbook. Hyperlinks can make it easier to navigate and access relevant information. Removing hyperlinks can help declutter your workbook and make it easier to read.

Step-by-Step Guide:

- Open your Excel workbook.
- Select the cell(s) where you want to add a hyperlink.
- Right-click on the cell(s) and select "Hyperlink" from the context menu.
- In the "Insert Hyperlink" dialog box, select the "Place in This Document" option to link to another part of the same workbook, or select "Existing File or Web Page" to link to an external source.
- Enter the URL or cell reference you want to link to.
- Click the "OK" button to save the hyperlink.

How to Remove a Hyperlink in Excel:

- Open your Excel workbook.
- Select the cell(s) containing the hyperlink you want to remove.
- Right-click on the cell(s) and select "Remove Hyperlink" from the context menu.
- The hyperlink will be removed from the cell(s).

Additional Tips:

- You can also add a hyperlink by pressing "Ctrl" + "K" on your keyboard.
- To edit an existing hyperlink, right-click on the cell(s) and select "Edit Hyperlink" from the context menu.
- Be careful when removing hyperlinks, as it permanently removes the hyperlink and its associated link.

Add Barcode

Adding a barcode to an Excel worksheet can make it easier to track inventory, prices, and other data. Barcodes are machine-readable symbols that represent data. When scanned, they can quickly and accurately identify a product or item.

Step-by-Step Guide:

- Determine the type of barcode you need: There are different types of barcodes, such as Code 39, Code 128, and UPC-A. Determine which type is appropriate for your needs.
- Install a barcode font: In order to generate barcodes, you need to install a barcode font. You can find these fonts online and download them to your computer.
- Enter the data: In the cell where you want the barcode to appear, enter the data that you want to encode. For example, if you're creating a barcode for an item, you might enter the item's SKU number.
- Apply the barcode font: Highlight the cell where you entered the data and select the barcode font you installed from the font drop-down menu.
- Generate the barcode: Once the font is applied, the data you entered should automatically generate a barcode. You can test the barcode by using a barcode scanner or reader to confirm that it can read the data accurately.
- To remove a barcode, simply delete the contents of the cell or change the font back to a regular font.

The exact steps may vary slightly depending on the version of Excel you are using and the specific barcode font you have installed.

Add Calculated Field and Item (Formulas in a Pivot Table)

A calculated field is a formula that you create in a pivot table. It uses the data in the pivot table and performs a calculation on it, such as adding or multiplying values. The calculated field is then displayed as a new column in the pivot table. A calculated item is similar to a calculated field, but it performs a calculation on an existing field in the pivot table, such as summing or averaging values for specific items.

Step-by-Step Guide:

- First, select a cell within your pivot table.
- Next, go to the "PivotTable Analyze" or "Options" tab on the Excel ribbon and select "Fields, Items & Sets."
- In the drop-down menu, select "Calculated Field" to create a new field or "Calculated Item" to create a new item.
- In the "Name" field, enter a name for your new field or item.
- In the "Formula" field, enter your formula using the appropriate syntax. For example, to add two fields together, you would enter "=field1 + field2."
- Click "Add" to create the new field or item.
- The new field or item will now appear in your pivot table as a new column or row, depending on your selection.

To delete a calculated field or item:

- Go to the "PivotTable Analyze" or "Options" tab on the Excel ribbon and select "Fields, Items & Sets."
- Select the calculated field or item you want to delete.
- Click "Delete" to remove it from the pivot table.

Add Column (Excel Shortcut)

Adding a column in Excel is a basic but essential task that can save you a lot of time. Using a shortcut to add a column can speed up your work process, especially if you are working with large datasets.

Step-by-Step Guide:

- Select the cell to the right of where you want to insert the new column.
- Press the "Ctrl" and "Shift" keys on your keyboard at the same time.
- While holding down both keys, press the "+" key.
- A "Insert" dialog box will appear. Choose "Entire column" and click "OK".
- The new column will be added to your worksheet.
- And that's it! You've successfully added a column using the Excel shortcut.

You can also add a column by right-clicking on a cell and selecting "Insert" from the context menu, then choosing "Entire column". However, using the keyboard shortcut is faster and more efficient, especially if you're working with a large dataset.

Add Hours to Time in Excel

Adding hours to time in Excel can be a useful function when working with time-based data, such as work schedules or project timelines. The function allows you to easily add a certain number of hours to a specific time value, which can save you time and reduce the risk of errors.

Step-by-Step Guide:

- Enter the time value in a cell. For example, if you want to add 4 hours to the time value of 9:00 AM, enter "9:00 AM" in a cell.
- Enter the number of hours you want to add in another cell. For example, if you want to add 4 hours, enter "4" in a cell.
- Select an empty cell where you want to display the result.
- Type the following formula: =TIME(HOUR(A1)+HOUR(B1),MINUTE(A1)+MINUTE(B1),SECOND(A1)+SECOND(B1))
- Replace A1 with the cell reference of the original time value (in this example, it would be the cell with "9:00 AM").
- Replace B1 with the cell reference of the number of hours you want to add (in this example, it would be the cell with "4").
- Press Enter to apply the formula and the result will appear in the selected cell.

Add Indent (Excel Shortcut)

Indentation in Excel allows you to move the content of a cell to the right or left, which is useful for creating a hierarchy or sub-categories in your data. By indenting the content, you can make your data more organized and easier to read.

Step-by-Step Guide:

- Select the cell or range of cells that you want to indent.
- Press the Alt + H keyboard shortcut keys together.
- Then press the O and I keys in sequence.
- Alternatively, you can right-click on the cell or range of cells and select "Format Cells" from the menu.
- In the Format Cells dialog box, go to the Alignment tab.
- In the Indent section, you can increase or decrease the indentation by clicking the Increase Indent or Decrease Indent buttons, respectively.
- You can also enter a specific number of characters to indent in the "Indent" box.
- Click OK to apply the changes.

Steps to Remove Indent:

- Select the cell or range of cells that you want to remove the indent from.
- Press the Alt + H keyboard shortcut keys together.
- Then press the O and L keys in sequence.
- Alternatively, you can right-click on the cell or range of cells and select "Format Cells" from the menu.

- In the Format Cells dialog box, go to the Alignment tab.
- In the Indent section, change the "Indent" box value to 0 (zero).
- Click OK to apply the changes.

Add Leading Zeros in Excel

Adding leading zeros in Excel is a formatting trick that adds zeros before a number so that it appears as a specified length. For example, if you have a list of IDs that are supposed to be seven digits long, but some are only five digits, adding leading zeros will ensure that all the IDs are the same length.

Step-by-Step Guide:

- Select the cells you want to add leading zeros to.
- Right-click on the selected cells and choose "Format Cells" from the menu that appears.
- In the "Format Cells" dialog box, select the "Custom" category.
- In the "Type" field, enter the number of zeros you want to add followed by the format code for the number you want to display. For example, if you want to display a seven-digit number with leading zeros, enter "0000000" as the format code.
- Click "OK" to apply the formatting.

Alternatively, you can use the TEXT function to add leading zeros to a number in a formula. The syntax for the TEXT function is:

=TEXT(value, format_text)

For example, if the number you want to add leading zeros to is in cell A1, and you want to display it as a seven-digit number with leading zeros, the formula would be:

=TEXT(A1, "0000000")

This will return the value in cell A1 with leading zeros added to make it a seven-digit number.

Add Minutes to Time in Excel

Adding minutes to time in Excel can be useful for tasks such as calculating time differences or adding/subtracting a specific amount of time from a given time.

Step-by-Step Guide:

- Open a new or existing Excel workbook.
- In a cell, enter the starting time that you want to add minutes to. For example, enter "9:00 AM" without quotes in cell A1.
- In the cell where you want the updated time to appear, enter the following formula: =A1 + TIME(0, minutes, 0). For example, if you want to add 30 minutes to the starting time in cell A1, you would enter the following formula in cell B1: =A1 + TIME(0, 30, 0).
- Press Enter to apply the formula. The updated time, with the added minutes, will appear in the cell you entered the formula into.

To break down the formula used in step 3:

- A1 is the cell containing the starting time.
- TIME(0, minutes, 0) is a function that adds the specified number of minutes to the starting time.
- The first argument (0) indicates that we don't want to add any hours.
- The second argument (minutes) is the number of minutes we want to add to the starting time.
- The third argument (0) indicates that we don't want to add any seconds.

Add Month to a Date in Excel

Adding months to a date in Excel can be helpful when you want to calculate future dates, such as payment due dates, project deadlines, or expiration dates.

Step-by-Step Guide:

- Enter the starting date in a cell, let's say cell A1.
- Enter the number of months you want to add in another cell, let's say cell B1.
- In a new cell, type the following formula: =EDATE(A1, B1)
- Press Enter, and the resulting cell will display the date that is X number of months after the starting date.

Add New Line in a Cell in Excel (Line Break)

Adding a new line in a cell in Excel allows you to split the content of the cell into multiple lines. This can make your data easier to read and organize, especially if you have long blocks of text or need to display data in a vertical list.

Step-by-Step Guide:

1. Select the cell in which you want to add a new line.
2. Click on the location within the cell where you want to insert the line break.
3. Press the keyboard shortcut Alt+Enter. Alternatively, you can press Ctrl+J on a Windows computer or Command+Option+Return on a Mac. This will add a line break at the selected location and move the cursor to the next line within the same cell.
4. Type in the text for the next line.
5. Repeat steps 2-4 to add additional lines as needed.

To remove a line break, simply delete the text between the two line breaks and press the delete key. This will merge the two lines back into one.

Add New Sheet (Excel Shortcut)

Adding new sheets in Excel can be very useful when working on large or complex workbooks. It helps to keep your data organized and makes it easier to navigate through your workbook.

Step-by-Step Guide:

- Open the Excel workbook in which you want to add a new sheet.
- Look for the plus sign (+) icon at the bottom left-hand corner of the screen. This is located next to the last sheet tab in your workbook.
- Right-click on the plus sign (+) icon.
- From the menu that appears, click on "Insert..."
- In the "Insert" dialog box that appears, select "Worksheet" and click "OK". This will add a new sheet to your workbook.
- Alternatively, you can use the keyboard shortcut "Shift + F11" to insert a new sheet directly without right-clicking on the plus sign (+) icon.

Add or Remove Grand Total in a Pivot Table in Excel

In a PivotTable, Grand Total is the sum of all values in the table. By default, the Grand Total row and column are displayed in a PivotTable. However, there may be situations where you want to remove the Grand Total, or add it to a specific row or column.

Step-by-Step Guide:

- Open the Excel workbook with the PivotTable you want to modify.
- Click anywhere inside the PivotTable to activate the PivotTable Tools tab.
- On the Design tab, go to the Layout group.
- To remove the Grand Total, uncheck the checkbox next to "Grand Totals" in the Layout group. This will remove the Grand Total row and column from the PivotTable.
- To add the Grand Total, first select the row or column where you want the Grand Total to appear. For example, if you want the Grand Total for a specific column, click on any cell in that column.
- In the Layout group, click on the drop-down menu next to "Grand Totals", and select "On for Rows" or "On for Columns", depending on where you want the Grand Total to appear.
- The Grand Total row or column will now appear in the PivotTable.

Add Ranks in Pivot Table in Excel

In Excel, a Pivot Table is a powerful tool that allows users to quickly summarize large amounts of data. One of the useful features of a Pivot Table is the ability to add ranks to the data. Ranks help to identify the top or bottom values in a field and provide insights into data trends.

Step-by-Step Guide:

- First, select any cell inside the Pivot Table.
- Then, navigate to the "PivotTable Analyze" tab in the Excel ribbon.
- Next, click on the "Fields, Items & Sets" button and select "Value Field Settings" from the drop-down menu.
- In the "Value Field Settings" dialog box, select the field for which you want to add ranks and click on the "Show Values As" tab.
- From the drop-down list, select "Rank Largest to Smallest" to show the largest values as rank 1 and the smallest values as the highest rank.
- Alternatively, you can select "Rank Smallest to Largest" to show the smallest values as rank 1 and the largest values as the highest rank.
- You can also choose to show the rank as a percentage by selecting "Rank Largest to Smallest %" or "Rank Smallest to Largest %".
- Click OK to apply the changes.
- Now, the Pivot Table will display a new column with the ranks for the selected field.

Note:

You can also add ranks for multiple fields in a Pivot Table by repeating the above steps for each field.

You can customize the rank format by going to the "Number Format" tab in the "Value Field Settings" dialog box.

If you want to remove the rank from the Pivot Table, simply go to the "Value Field Settings" dialog box and select "None" from the "Show Values As" tab.

Add Running Total in a Pivot Table in Excel

Adding a running total to a Pivot Table in Excel helps in showing the accumulated value of data as it progresses through time. A running total is useful when you want to see how a particular field in the table changes as it accumulates over a period.

Step-by-Step Guide:

- Select any cell within the Pivot Table where you want to add a running total.
- Go to the "Value Field Settings" option in the "Values" tab in the "PivotTable Fields" window.
- In the "Value Field Settings" dialog box, select "Running Total In" under the "Show Values As" tab.
- Select the field you want to show the running total for from the drop-down list next to "Base Field."
- Select the field you want to group by from the drop-down list next to "Base Item."
- Click "OK" to close the dialog box.
- The running total will now appear as a new column in your Pivot Table.

The running total will be displayed based on the field and grouping that you selected in the above steps. You can repeat the above steps for each field in the Pivot Table that you want to add a running total for.

Add Secondary Axis in Excel Charts

Adding a secondary axis in an Excel chart allows the user to plot two different data series with different scales on the same chart. This can be particularly useful when comparing data sets that have different units of measurement or ranges.

Step-by-Step Guide:

- First, create a chart with two data series that you want to compare. Select the chart by clicking on it.
- Go to the "Chart Design" tab in the Excel ribbon menu.
- Click on the "Change Chart Type" button.
- In the "Change Chart Type" dialog box, select the chart type that you want to use for the second data series (e.g. line chart).
- In the "Chart sub-type" section, choose the chart sub-type that has a secondary axis (e.g. Line with Markers and Secondary Axis).
- Click on "OK" to close the "Change Chart Type" dialog box. You will now see that the second data series has been added to the chart with a secondary axis.
- Select the secondary axis by clicking on it.
- In the "Format" tab, click on "Format Selection" to open the "Format Axis" pane.
- Under the "Axis Options" section, choose the "Secondary Axis" radio button.
- Adjust the formatting of the secondary axis as needed (e.g. change the scale, format the axis labels).
- Click on "Close" to close the "Format Axis" pane.

Your chart should now have a secondary axis that allows you to compare two data series with different scales.

Add Serial Numbers

Adding serial numbers to data in Excel is a useful trick to keep track of the data and quickly identify each row's unique identifier. It is particularly helpful when dealing with large amounts of data, as it makes it easier to sort and filter the data. In this trick, we will add serial numbers to the data using the Excel "ROW" function.

Step-by-Step Guide:

- Open the Excel sheet containing the data you want to add serial numbers to.
- Click on the cell where you want to start the serial number.
- Type "=ROW()" in the formula bar without quotes and press enter. This will display the current row number in the selected cell.
- Copy the formula by pressing Ctrl+C or by right-clicking on the cell and selecting "Copy".
- Select the range of cells where you want to add serial numbers.
- Right-click on the selected cells and click on "Paste Special".
- In the "Paste Special" dialog box, select "Values" and click on "OK". This will replace the formula with the actual row numbers.
- If you want to start the serial number from a specific number (other than the first row number), subtract the starting number from the "ROW" function. For example, if you want to start the serial number from 100, type "=ROW()-99" in the formula bar and press enter.

To remove serial numbers from the data, select the range of cells containing the serial numbers and press the

"Delete" key or use the "Clear All" command from the "Home" tab in the ribbon.

Add Watermark in Excel

Adding a watermark to an Excel worksheet or document can help to clearly identify the status or purpose of the document, such as "draft" or "confidential". Watermarks can also help to prevent unauthorized distribution or copying of the document.

Step-by-Step Guide:

- Open the Excel worksheet or document you want to add a watermark to.
- Click on the "Page Layout" tab in the ribbon at the top of the Excel window.
- In the "Page Setup" section, click on the "Watermark" button.
- A drop-down menu will appear with several preset watermarks to choose from, such as "Confidential" or "Draft". Select the watermark you want to use by clicking on it.
- If you want to create a custom watermark, select "Custom Watermark" from the bottom of the drop-down menu.
- In the "Printed Watermark" dialog box that appears, select "Picture Watermark" and then click on the "Select Picture" button.
- Choose the image file you want to use as the watermark and then click "Insert".
- Choose the scale and washout options for the watermark as desired, and then click "OK" to close the "Printed Watermark" dialog box.

Your watermark will now appear on every page of the Excel worksheet or document. If you need to remove the watermark, simply follow the same steps and select "No Watermark" from the drop-down menu or uncheck the

"Picture Watermark" option in the "Printed Watermark" dialog box.

Add Years to Date in Excel

Adding years to a date in Excel allows you to quickly calculate a future date by adding a certain number of years to an existing date. This can be useful in financial planning, project management, and other applications where future dates need to be calculated.

Step-by-Step Guide:

- Open a new or existing Excel spreadsheet.
- Enter the starting date in a cell. For example, type "01/01/2022" in cell A1.
- In the cell where you want to display the future date, enter the formula "=DATE(YEAR(A1)+5, MONTH(A1), DAY(A1))". This formula adds 5 years to the date in cell A1. You can replace the "5" with any number of years you want to add.
- Press "Enter" to display the future date.

You can now see the future date that corresponds to the original date plus the number of years you added. You can repeat this process with different numbers of years and starting dates as needed.

Add-Subtract Week from a Date in Excel

Adding or subtracting weeks from a date in Excel can be useful when working with dates and timelines. For example, it can help in project management when you need to add or subtract a certain number of weeks from a start or end date.

Step-by-Step Guide:

- Select the cell where you want to display the result.
- Type an equal sign (=) to start the formula.
- Enter the date you want to add or subtract weeks from. For example, if you want to add or subtract weeks from cell A1, enter A1.
- Type a plus sign (+) if you want to add weeks or a minus sign (-) if you want to subtract weeks.
- Type the number of weeks you want to add or subtract. For example, if you want to add two weeks, enter 2. If you want to subtract three weeks, enter -3.
- Type the letter "w" to indicate that the number you entered is in weeks.
- Press the Enter key to calculate the result.

Here is an example formula: =A1+2w

This formula will add two weeks to the date in cell A1.

Make sure that the date in the cell you are referencing is in a proper date format. If it is not, Excel will not recognize it as a date and the formula will not work.

Align Center (Excel Shortcut)

In Excel, aligning the text or values to the center of a cell can make the content of the cell more visually appealing and easier to read. Instead of manually selecting the center alignment option from the menu, there is a keyboard shortcut that allows you to align cell contents to the center of the cell quickly and efficiently.

Step-by-Step Guide:

- Select the cell or range of cells that you want to align to the center.
- Press and hold the "Alt" key on your keyboard.
- While holding the "Alt" key, press the "H" key on your keyboard.
- Then, release both the keys and press the "A" key on your keyboard.
- Your text or values will now be aligned to the center of the selected cell(s).

You can also use the "Ctrl + 1" keyboard shortcut to open the Format Cells dialog box, where you can set the alignment to center, as well as other formatting options.

Apply Accounting Number Format in Excel

The "Accounting Number Format" is a way to format cells in Excel to display numbers in a way that is commonly used in financial statements. This format adds a currency symbol, aligns decimals, and includes parenthesis for negative numbers. It is particularly useful when dealing with monetary data.

Step-by-Step Guide:

- Select the cells that you want to format. You can do this by clicking on the first cell and dragging your cursor to select the rest of the cells.
- Right-click on the selected cells and choose "Format Cells" from the context menu. Alternatively, you can use the keyboard shortcut "Ctrl+1" (hold down the Ctrl key and press 1).
- In the "Format Cells" dialog box, select the "Accounting" category from the list on the left.
- Choose the options that you want for the format. For example, you can select a specific symbol from the dropdown menu, choose the number of decimal places to display, and specify how negative numbers should be displayed.
- Click "OK" to apply the Accounting Number Format to the selected cells.

The selected cells will now display numbers in the Accounting Number Format. This format can also be applied to specific parts of a worksheet or to an entire column by selecting the appropriate cells before applying the format.

Apply and Remove Filter (Excel Shortcut)

The trick we will learn in this guide is how to apply and remove filters in Excel using a keyboard shortcut. Filters allow you to sort and organize data in a spreadsheet based on specific criteria, making it easier to work with large amounts of information.

Step-by-Step Guide:

- To apply a filter, select any cell within the range of data you want to filter.
- Press the keyboard shortcut Ctrl + Shift + L. This will apply the filter to your selected range.
- To remove the filter, select any cell within your filtered range.
- Press the keyboard shortcut Ctrl + Shift + L again. This will remove the filter from your selected range.
- You can also apply and remove filters by going to the "Data" tab in the Excel ribbon and clicking on the "Filter" button.

With this keyboard shortcut, you can quickly apply and remove filters in Excel, saving you time and making it easier to work with your data.

Apply and Remove Filter (Excel Shortcut)

Filtering data in Excel is a way to display only the data that meets specific criteria. The Filter function allows you to select a range of cells and display only the rows that meet certain conditions. This can help you find and analyze the data you need quickly and easily.

Applying and removing filters using a keyboard shortcut can save time and streamline your workflow.

Step-by-Step Guide:

- Select the range of cells that you want to filter.
- Press the keyboard shortcut "Ctrl + Shift + L". This will apply the filter to the selected range.
- You will see drop-down arrows appear in the header row of the selected cells, indicating that filters have been applied.

Steps to Remove Filter using Excel Shortcut:

- Select the range of cells that you want to remove filters from.
- Press the keyboard shortcut "Ctrl + Shift + L" again. This will remove the filters from the selected range.
- The drop-down arrows will disappear from the header row, indicating that filters have been removed.

The shortcut "Ctrl + Shift + L" can also be accessed via the "Data" tab on the Excel ribbon.

Apply Border (Excel Shortcut)

In Excel, borders are used to highlight cells, columns, and rows. They help to differentiate the data and provide a structured look to the worksheet. Applying borders to cells and ranges in Excel is a common task that can be done in several ways.

Step-by-Step Guide:

- Open the Excel worksheet where you want to apply borders.
- Select the cell or range of cells where you want to apply the border.
- To apply a border to the entire cell, press the "Ctrl + Shift + 7" keys simultaneously. If you want to apply a specific border, such as a top border, a bottom border, or a diagonal border, you can use the following Excel shortcuts:
- Top border: "Ctrl + Shift + Underscore (_)"
- Bottom border: "Ctrl + Shift + Hyphen (-)"
- Left border: "Ctrl + Shift + Ampersand (&)"
- Right border: "Ctrl + Shift + Plus (+)"
- Diagonal border: "Ctrl + Shift + Forward Slash (/)"
- To apply a double border, use the "Ctrl + Shift + 5" shortcut.
- To apply a thick border, use the "Ctrl + Shift + 9" shortcut.
- To apply an outline border to a range of cells, use the "Ctrl + Shift + ampersand (&)" shortcut.
- To apply an outside border to a range of cells, use the "Ctrl + Shift + pipe (|)" shortcut.
- To remove a border, select the cell or range of cells and press the "Ctrl + Shift + Underscore (_)" shortcut.

These shortcuts work in Windows. For Mac, use the "Command" key instead of the "Ctrl" key.

Apply Comma Style in Excel

The "Comma Style" is a number format in Excel that adds thousand separators to numbers and rounds them to a specified number of decimal places. This can make large numbers easier to read and understand, especially in financial and accounting contexts.

Step-by-Step Guide:

- Select the cell or range of cells that you want to apply the format to.
- Right-click on the selection and choose "Format Cells" from the dropdown menu, or go to the "Home" tab in the Excel ribbon and click on the "Number Format" dropdown.
- In the "Format Cells" dialog box, select "Number" in the category list.
- In the "Number" tab, select "Comma" in the "Number style" list.
- If desired, adjust the number of decimal places by using the up and down arrows in the "Decimal places" box or by entering a number directly.
- Click "OK" to apply the format.

To remove the "Comma Style" from a cell or range of cells:

- Select the cell or range of cells that you want to remove the format from.
- Right-click on the selection and choose "Format Cells" from the dropdown menu, or go to the "Home" tab in the Excel ribbon and click on the "Number Format" dropdown.
- In the "Format Cells" dialog box, select "General" in the category list.
- Click "OK" to remove the format.

Apply Conditional Formatting to a Pivot Table

Conditional formatting is a powerful tool in Excel that allows you to highlight certain values or cells based on specific conditions. When applied to a pivot table, it can help you quickly identify important trends and patterns in your data.

Step-by-Step Guide:

- Open your Excel workbook and navigate to the worksheet containing the pivot table you want to format.
- Select any cell within the pivot table, and then go to the Home tab in the ribbon.
- Click on the "Conditional Formatting" button in the Styles group, and then select "Highlight Cell Rules" from the drop-down menu.
- Choose one of the options such as "Greater Than," "Less Than," or "Between" depending on the criteria you want to apply.
- Enter the appropriate values in the boxes provided. For example, if you choose "Greater Than," you will need to enter the minimum value that you want to highlight.
- Choose the formatting style you want to apply to the highlighted cells. For example, you could choose to highlight the cells in red or yellow, or you could choose to bold the text in the cells.
- Click "OK" to apply the conditional formatting to the pivot table.
- To remove conditional formatting, simply select any cell in the pivot table, and then click on the "Conditional Formatting" button in the Styles group on the Home tab.

- Choose "Clear Rules" from the drop-down menu, and then select "Clear Rules from Entire PivotTable."
- Click "OK" to remove the conditional formatting from the pivot table.

Apply Date Format (Excel Shortcut)

Excel allows you to format dates in a variety of ways, including applying date formats to cells using shortcuts. Applying date formats helps to improve the readability and organization of your data by displaying dates in a clear and consistent format. By using the Excel shortcut to apply date formats, you can save time and simplify the process of formatting dates in your spreadsheet.

Step-by-Step Guide:

- Open the Excel sheet where you want to apply date format.
- Select the cell or range of cells that contain the dates you want to format.
- Press the "Ctrl + 1" shortcut key. This will open the Format Cells dialog box.
- In the Format Cells dialog box, select the "Number" tab.
- Under "Category," select "Date."
- From the "Type" list, select the desired date format that you want to apply.
- Once you've selected your desired date format, click "OK" to apply the format to the selected cell(s).

The selected cell(s) should now be formatted with your desired date format.

If the selected cell(s) don't show up in the desired format, check to make sure the cell(s) are not formatted as text. To fix this, you can select the cell(s) and change the format to "General" in the Format Cells dialog box, then reapply the date format as described above.

Apply Multiple Filters to Columns

Excel provides a powerful feature called "Filtering" that allows users to view specific data in a worksheet quickly. With filtering, users can display only the data they want to see by hiding the rows that don't meet certain criteria.

Step-by-Step Guide:

- Open the Excel worksheet with the data you want to filter.
- Select the column header(s) for which you want to apply the filter(s).
- On the Home tab, click on the "Filter" button in the "Editing" group. Alternatively, you can use the keyboard shortcut "Ctrl+Shift+L."
- Once the filter is applied, click on the drop-down arrow on the column header to display the filter menu.
- To apply multiple filters, click on "Filter by Color," "Filter by Cell Color," or "Filter by Font Color" to filter by color, or "Text Filters," "Number Filters," or "Date Filters" to filter by text, number, or date.
- Choose the filter options that you want to apply to each column. You can choose multiple filter options at once.
- Click "OK" to apply the filters.
- To remove the filters, click on the "Filter" button on the "Data" tab again or use the keyboard shortcut "Ctrl+Shift+L."

Apply Print Titles in Excel (Set Row 1 to Print on Every Page)

When you have a large Excel worksheet that spans multiple pages when printed, it can be helpful to have certain rows or columns repeat on every printed page. One common example of this is having the header row (usually row 1) repeat on each page, so that users can easily see what the columns represent. This is where applying print titles in Excel comes in handy.

Step-by-Step Guide:

- Open the Excel worksheet that you want to apply print titles to.
- Select the Page Layout tab from the ribbon at the top of the screen.
- Click on the Print Titles button, located in the Page Setup group.
- In the Page Setup dialog box that appears, click on the Sheet tab.
- In the Rows to repeat at top box, click on the small icon to the right.
- In the worksheet, select row 1.
- Press Enter or click on the icon with the checkmark to the right of the box.
- Click OK to close the Page Setup dialog box.
- To preview the print titles, click on the File tab and select Print.
- Verify that row 1 is set to repeat on every page in the preview pane.

To remove print titles, simply follow steps 1-3 above, and then clear the Rows to repeat at top box by clicking on the small icon to the right and selecting the appropriate rows to remove. Click OK to close the Page Setup dialog box and apply the changes.

Apply Time Format (Excel Shortcut)

Excel is a powerful tool that allows you to manipulate and analyze data. One of the important features of Excel is the ability to format cells to display data in a desired way. Time format is one such feature in Excel that enables you to display time values in a specific format. You can use the time format to display time in various formats such as hours, minutes, seconds, and milliseconds.

Step-by-Step Guide:

Here's how you can apply the time format in Excel using the shortcut:

- Select the cell(s) that you want to format.
- Press the "Ctrl" and "1" keys on your keyboard simultaneously. This will open the "Format Cells" dialog box.
- In the "Number" tab, select "Time" from the "Category" list.
- Choose the format that you want from the "Type" list. You can preview the different formats in the "Sample" section.
- Click "OK" to apply the format to the selected cell(s).

To remove the time format from a cell, you can follow these steps:

- Select the cell(s) that you want to remove the time format from.
- Press the "Ctrl" and "1" keys on your keyboard simultaneously to open the "Format Cells" dialog box.

- In the "Number" tab, select "General" from the "Category" list.
- Click "OK" to remove the time format from the selected cell(s).

Auto Fit (Excel Shortcut)

One of the most important aspects of creating a professional-looking Excel worksheet is to ensure that all the content fits within the cells properly. Sometimes, the cell contents may be too long, causing them to spill over into the adjacent cells, making the sheet look cluttered and disorganized. The solution to this problem is to use the AutoFit feature in Excel, which automatically adjusts the width of the column to fit the content.

Step-by-Step Guide:

- Open the Excel worksheet that you want to format.
- Select the column or columns that you want to AutoFit. You can do this by clicking on the column letter(s) at the top of the sheet.
- Double-click on the right-hand side of any selected column header. This will automatically adjust the column width to fit the widest content in that column.
- Alternatively, you can click on the Home tab on the Excel ribbon and then click on the Format button in the Cells group.
- From the drop-down menu, select AutoFit Column Width.
- The column(s) will be automatically adjusted to fit the content.

Steps to Apply AutoFit in Excel Using Shortcut Key:

- Open the Excel worksheet that you want to format.

- Select the column or columns that you want to AutoFit. You can do this by clicking on the column letter(s) at the top of the sheet.
- Use the shortcut key combination "Alt + H + O + I" on your keyboard.
- The column(s) will be automatically adjusted to fit the content.

AutoFormat

AutoFormat is a feature in Excel that allows you to quickly apply a pre-designed formatting style to your data. With just a few clicks, you can change the font, color, and alignment of your data to create a more professional and polished look.

Step-by-Step Guide:

- Open the worksheet containing the data you want to format.
- Select the range of cells you want to format.
- Go to the "Home" tab in the Excel ribbon.
- Click the "Format as Table" button in the "Styles" group.
- Select a table style from the drop-down menu.
- If you have headers in your data, make sure the "My table has headers" checkbox is selected.
- Click "OK" to apply the formatting to your data.

You can also access AutoFormat by going to the "Format" menu, selecting "AutoFormat", and then choosing a formatting style from the list.

AutoSum (Excel Shortcut)

AutoSum is a popular Excel shortcut that allows you to quickly add up a range of numbers in a column or row. Instead of manually typing a formula to add up the values, AutoSum automatically detects the range of cells to be summed and generates the formula for you.

Step-by-Step Guide:

- Open an Excel spreadsheet and navigate to the cell where you want to display the sum.
- Click on the cell to select it.
- Press the "Alt" key on your keyboard and then press the "=" key. This will activate the AutoSum function.
- Excel will automatically detect the range of cells that appear to be adjacent to the selected cell and highlight them.
- If the detected range is correct, simply press the "Enter" key on your keyboard to complete the formula and display the sum in the selected cell.
- If the detected range is incorrect, use your mouse to adjust the range by clicking and dragging to highlight the desired cells.
- Once the desired range is selected, press the "Enter" key to complete the formula and display the sum in the selected cell.

Average TOP 5 Values in Excel

The AVERAGE function in Excel is a widely used statistical function that calculates the average value of a range of cells. The AVERAGE function can also be used to calculate the average of the top or bottom values in a range of cells. This is useful when you want to analyze data and focus on the most important information.

Step-by-Step Guide:

- Enter your data into an Excel worksheet.
- Select the cell where you want to display the average of the top 5 values.
- Type the following formula into the cell: =AVERAGE(LARGE(range,1),LARGE(range,2), LARGE(range,3),LARGE(range,4),LARGE(range ,5))
- Replace "range" with the range of cells you want to calculate the average of the top 5 values for.
- Press Enter on your keyboard.
- The cell should now display the average of the top 5 values in the range of cells you specified.

Note that if there are less than 5 values in the range, the formula will return an error.

Bullet Points

Bullet points are a useful way to organize and present information in a clear and concise manner. They can be used to break down complex information into easy-to-read lists that are visually appealing.

Step-by-Step Guide:

- Select the cell where you want to insert bullet points.
- Go to the "Home" tab in the Excel ribbon.
- Click on the "Wrap Text" button to ensure that the cell contents wrap within the cell.
- Click on the "Bullet Points" button, which is located in the "Paragraph" group.
- A bullet point will be inserted into the selected cell. Type in your first bullet point and press "Enter" to move to the next line.
- Press the "Tab" key to indent and create a sub-level bullet point.
- Type in your sub-level bullet point and press "Enter" to move to the next line.
- Repeat steps 6 and 7 to add more sub-level bullet points.
- Press "Enter" twice to create a new line without a bullet point.
- To stop using bullet points, press "Backspace" until the bullet point disappears or click on the "Bullet Points" button again to turn it off.

Calculate Compound Interest in Excel

Compound interest is the interest that is added to the principal amount and the interest that has already been accumulated on that principal amount. In simpler terms, it is interest on interest. Excel can be used to calculate compound interest easily, accurately, and quickly.

Step-by-Step Guide:

- Open a new or existing Excel worksheet.
- Decide on the values you want to use for the principal amount, interest rate, and time period. Enter these values in the appropriate cells.
- In a blank cell, enter the formula for calculating compound interest: =P*(1+r/n)^(n*t)-P where P is the principal amount, r is the interest rate, n is the number of times interest is compounded in a year, and t is the time period in years.
- Replace the letters P, r, n, and t in the formula with the cell references containing the values for the principal amount, interest rate, number of compounding periods, and time period respectively.
- Press Enter to calculate the compound interest.

Calculate Cube Root in Excel

Excel is not just a simple spreadsheet program. It is equipped with a lot of mathematical functions that can help you do complex calculations quickly and easily. One such function is the CUBEROOT function, which calculates the cube root of a given number. This function can be useful for anyone who needs to calculate cube roots regularly, such as students, researchers, and analysts.

Step-by-Step Guide:

- Open a new or existing Excel spreadsheet.
- Select the cell where you want to display the result.
- Type the following formula in the cell: =CUBEROOT(number)
- Replace "number" with the actual value or cell reference for which you want to find the cube root.
- Press enter to calculate the cube root.
- The result will appear in the cell you selected.

Tips:

- You can also use the CUBEROOT function in combination with other Excel functions to perform more complex calculations.
- Make sure that you enter the correct number or cell reference in the formula, or else you will get an error.
- Use the "Format Cells" option to change the format of the result if necessary.
- You can copy and paste the formula to other cells to calculate multiple cube roots at once. Just make sure to update the cell references accordingly.

The CUBEROOT function is only available in Excel 2010 or later versions. If you have an older version of Excel, you can still calculate cube roots using a formula based on the POWER function.

Calculate Percentage Variance (Difference) in Excel

Calculating percentage variance or difference is a useful tool for analyzing changes in values over time or between different scenarios. It measures the percentage change between two numbers and helps in understanding how much a value has increased or decreased relative to the starting value. In Excel, you can easily calculate percentage variance using a simple formula.

Step-by-Step Guide:

- Enter the starting value in cell A1.
- Enter the ending value in cell B1.
- In cell C1, enter the formula: =(B1-A1)/A1.
- Press enter and the result will be displayed as a decimal value.
- To convert the decimal value into a percentage, select cell C1 and right-click on it.
- Select the "Format Cells" option from the drop-down menu.
- In the Format Cells dialog box, select "Percentage" from the Category list.
- Set the number of decimal places to the desired value (e.g. 0 or 2).
- Click "OK" to apply the formatting and the result will be displayed as a percentage.

The formula can also be written as =(B1/A1)-1 to get the same result.

Calculate Simple Interest in Excel

Calculating interest is a common task in finance, and it can be done easily using Excel. Simple interest is a type of interest that is calculated only on the principal amount. It is a straightforward method of calculating interest, which makes it useful for short-term loans or financial instruments.

Step-by-Step Guide:

- Open a new Excel sheet and enter the following headings in cells A1, B1, C1, D1, and E1 respectively: "Principal", "Rate", "Time", "Interest", and "Total Amount".
- Enter the values for the principal, rate, and time in cells A2, B2, and C2, respectively.
- In cell D2, enter the formula for calculating the interest: "=A2B2C2"
- In cell E2, enter the formula for calculating the total amount: "=A2+D2"
- Format the interest and total amount cells as currency by selecting the cells and clicking on the "Currency" button in the "Number" tab.
- Now, you can change the values of the principal, rate, and time to see how they affect the interest and total amount.

Calculate the Age

Calculating age in Excel can be a useful tool when working with data that includes birth dates. It can help to analyze data such as customer demographics, employee records, and more. By using the DATEDIF function in Excel, you can easily calculate the age of a person based on their birth date.

Step-by-Step Guide:

- Open a new or existing Excel worksheet where you want to perform the calculation.
- In a cell where you want to display the age, type "=DATEDIF(" without the quotes.
- Next, enter the birth date of the person you want to calculate the age for, in this format "birthdate," where "birthdate" is the cell reference where the birth date is stored. For example, if the birth date is in cell A2, enter "A2," without the quotes.
- Enter a comma "," after the birthdate.
- Enter the word "today()" without quotes after the comma. This function will calculate the age as of today's date.
- Enter a comma "," after the "today()" function.
- Enter "y" as the unit to calculate the age in years, "m" for months, or "d" for days.
- Close the formula with a closing bracket ")" and press enter.

Your age formula should now look something like this: =DATEDIF(A2,today(), "y")

And it will display the age of the person in years based on today's date.

If you want to calculate the age as of a specific date, you can replace the "today()" function with a specific date enclosed in quotes in the format "mm/dd/yyyy".

Calculate the Coefficient of Variation (CV) in Excel

The Coefficient of Variation (CV) is a statistical measure used to measure the relative variability of a dataset. It is calculated as the ratio of the standard deviation to the mean of a dataset, and is expressed as a percentage. The CV is a useful measure for comparing the variability of different datasets that have different means.

Step-by-Step Guide:

- Enter your dataset in a column in Excel.
- Calculate the mean of the dataset using the AVERAGE function.
- Calculate the standard deviation of the dataset using the STDEV.S function.
- Divide the standard deviation by the mean and multiply by 100 to get the CV percentage. Use the following formula in a cell: =STDEV.S(A1:A10)/AVERAGE(A1:A10)*100 (replace A1:A10 with the range of cells containing your dataset).

Calculate the Ratio

In Excel, you can calculate the ratio between two values using a simple formula. The ratio can be expressed as a percentage, decimal or fraction. Ratios are used in many applications, such as financial analysis, comparing performance metrics, and calculating probabilities.

Step-by-Step Guide:

- Enter the two values you want to compare in separate cells.
- Decide how you want to express the ratio (as a percentage, decimal or fraction).
- In a new cell, type the "=" sign to begin the formula.
- Click on the cell containing the first value in the ratio.
- Type the division symbol "/".
- Click on the cell containing the second value in the ratio.
- Press Enter to complete the formula.
- If you want to express the ratio as a percentage, format the cell as a percentage by selecting the cell and pressing Ctrl+Shift+%.

Calculate the Weighted Average in Excel

Calculating the weighted average is an important statistical calculation that assigns different weights to different values based on their importance or relevance. This is particularly useful when calculating a grade or a final score, where certain assignments or exams may be worth more than others. In Excel, you can easily calculate the weighted average using a formula that takes into account both the values and their corresponding weights.

Step-by-Step Guide:

- First, create a new column in your spreadsheet to calculate the weighted values. This column should be placed immediately next to the column containing the values you want to average.
- In the first cell of the weighted value column, enter the formula "=value*weight". Replace "value" with the cell reference of the corresponding value, and "weight" with the cell reference of the weight assigned to that value.
- Copy this formula to all of the cells in the weighted value column, so that each value is multiplied by its corresponding weight.
- Next, sum up the total weighted values in the column using the "SUM" formula. To do this, select the cell below the last weighted value and enter the formula "=SUM(first_cell:last_cell)", where "first_cell" is the cell reference of the first weighted value and "last_cell" is the cell reference of the last weighted value.
- Finally, divide the total weighted value by the sum of the weights to get the weighted average. To do this, select the cell where you want to display the weighted average and enter the formula "=total_weighted_value/sum_of_weights", where

"total_weighted_value" is the cell reference of the total weighted value calculated in step 4, and "sum_of_weights" is the sum of the weights for all values in the dataset.

Calculate Time Difference Between Two Times in Excel

Calculating the time difference between two times can be a challenging task, especially if you need to do it manually. However, with Excel, you can easily calculate the time difference between two times using a simple formula.

Step-by-Step Guide:

- Enter the start time in one cell and the end time in another cell. Make sure to use the correct format for the time, which is "hh:mm:ss AM/PM".
- In a third cell, subtract the start time from the end time using the following formula: = end time - start time
- The result will be displayed as a decimal number, which represents the time difference in days and fractions of a day. To convert the result to a time format, select the cell and change the number format to "hh:mm:ss".
- You can also add a label to the cell to indicate what the result represents, such as "Duration" or "Time Difference".

Capitalize First Letter in Excel

Capitalizing the first letter of a word is a common formatting requirement in Excel. It helps to make the text look neat and tidy, especially in titles, headings, or other important cells.

Step-by-Step Guide:

- Open the Excel spreadsheet containing the text you want to capitalize.
- Select the cell or cells containing the text you want to capitalize.
- In the formula bar, type the following formula: =PROPER(A1)
- *A1 is the cell reference of the cell you want to capitalize. If you selected multiple cells, the formula will be applied to all of them at once.
- Press Enter.
- The first letter of each word in the selected cell(s) will now be capitalized.
- To apply the formula to other cells, simply copy and paste the formula into the desired cell(s).

Cell Message

In Excel, you can add messages to cells to provide additional information about the data entered in the cell. These messages can be used to indicate the type of data that should be entered in the cell, provide warnings or alerts about the data, or give instructions to the user.

Step-by-Step Guide:

- Select the cell where you want to add a message.
- Right-click on the cell and select "Format Cells" from the drop-down menu.
- In the Format Cells dialog box, click on the "Alignment" tab.
- Under the "Text control" section, check the box next to "Wrap text" and "Shrink to fit".
- Click on the "OK" button to close the dialog box.
- Hover your mouse over the border of the cell until you see a small red triangle in the top right corner of the cell.
- Click on the red triangle to display the message box.
- In the message box, enter the message you want to display.
- Click outside the message box to close it and save the message.

Cell Style (Title, Calculation, Total, Headings...) in Excel

Excel is a powerful tool that can be used for a wide range of tasks, from simple data entry to complex financial analysis. One of the key features of Excel is the ability to format cells in a variety of ways.

Step-by-Step Guide:

- Open your Excel spreadsheet and select the cells that you want to format with a cell style.
- Go to the "Home" tab in the Excel ribbon at the top of the screen.
- In the "Styles" section of the ribbon, click on the drop-down arrow next to "Cell Styles".
- Choose the type of cell style that you want to apply to your selected cells. There are several built-in cell styles to choose from, such as "Title", "Calculation", "Total", and "Heading".
- If you don't see a cell style that meets your needs, you can create a custom cell style by clicking on the "New Cell Style" option at the bottom of the drop-down menu.
- In the "Style" dialog box that appears, you can customize the cell style by selecting various formatting options, such as font, borders, and shading.
- Once you have created your custom cell style, you can apply it to your selected cells by going back to the "Cell Styles" drop-down menu and selecting your new style from the list.
- If you want to modify or delete a cell style, you can do so by clicking on the "Cell Styles" drop-down menu, right-clicking on the style you want

to modify or delete, and selecting the appropriate option.

Center a Worksheet Horizontally and Vertically in Excel

Centering a worksheet in Excel is a useful formatting technique to make it look more professional and presentable. You can center a worksheet horizontally, vertically, or both.

Step-by-Step Guide:

- Open the Excel workbook and select the worksheet that you want to center.
- To center the worksheet horizontally, click on the "Page Layout" tab in the ribbon at the top of the screen.
- In the "Page Setup" group, click on the "Margins" drop-down menu and select "Custom Margins".
- In the "Page Setup" dialog box, select the "Margins" tab.
- Under "Center on page", check the box next to "Horizontally".
- Click "OK" to close the dialog box and apply the changes.
- To center the worksheet vertically, click on the "Page Layout" tab again.
- In the "Page Setup" group, click on the "Dialog Box Launcher" button in the bottom right corner.
- In the "Page Setup" dialog box, select the "Page" tab.
- Under "Center on page", check the box next to "Vertically".
- Click "OK" to close the dialog box and apply the changes.
- To center the worksheet both horizontally and vertically, follow steps 1-6 and 7-11.

If you have any headers or footers in your worksheet, they may also be centered after following these steps. To adjust the header and footer alignment, go to the "Header/Footer" tab in the "Page Setup" dialog box and make changes as necessary.

Change Column to Row (Vice Versa) in Excel

Sometimes, you may need to switch the orientation of your data, such as changing columns to rows or rows to columns, to better analyze or present your data. Excel has a simple feature that allows you to quickly change columns to rows or vice versa, without having to copy and paste your data.

Step-by-Step Guide:

- Open the Excel workbook that contains the data you want to change.
- Select the column(s) or row(s) that you want to change. You can select multiple columns or rows by holding down the "Ctrl" key on your keyboard while clicking on each column or row.
- Right-click on the selected column(s) or row(s) and choose "Copy" from the drop-down menu, or press "Ctrl + C" on your keyboard to copy the selected data.
- Right-click on the cell where you want to paste the transposed data and choose "Paste Special" from the drop-down menu.
- In the "Paste Special" dialog box, check the "Transpose" option located in the lower-left corner of the dialog box.
- Click the "OK" button to transpose the data. Your columns will now be rows, and your rows will be columns.

Change Date Format in Excel

Excel provides various formats for representing date and time values. Changing the date format is essential when dealing with different datasets that might have different date formats. For instance, if you import data from an external source, the date format might not be compatible with your existing Excel worksheet. Therefore, knowing how to change the date format is an important skill for working with Excel.

Step-by-Step Guide:

- Select the cells with dates that you want to change the format for.
- Right-click on the selected cells and click on "Format Cells" or press "Ctrl + 1" to open the "Format Cells" dialog box.
- In the "Format Cells" dialog box, select the "Number" tab.
- In the "Category" list, select "Date" to display the available date formats.
- In the "Type" list, select the format that you want to apply to your date values. You can preview the format in the "Sample" section.
- Click "OK" to apply the selected date format to the selected cells.
- If you don't find the desired date format, you can create your own custom format by selecting "Custom" in the "Category" list and typing the desired format in the "Type" field. For example, "dd/mm/yyyy" or "yyyy-mm-dd".

Change Time Format in Excel

Changing the time format in Excel involves modifying the way time values are displayed. By default, Excel uses the "h:mm:ss AM/PM" format to display time values. However, sometimes you may want to change this format to better suit your needs or to match a particular format required by your organization or clients. Changing the time format can also make it easier to work with time values in Excel, especially when dealing with large amounts of data.

Step-by-Step Guide:

- Select the cell or range of cells containing the time values that you want to change the format for.
- Right-click on the selected cell(s) and click on "Format Cells" in the context menu that appears.
- In the "Format Cells" dialog box, click on the "Number" tab.
- In the "Category" list, select "Time" (or "Custom" if you want to create a custom time format).
- In the "Type" list, select the time format that you want to use. You can also create a custom time format by typing the format code in the "Type" box.
- Click "OK" to apply the new time format to the selected cell(s).

Chart Formatting

Charts are a powerful tool in Excel that allow users to visually represent data. However, it is important to format charts correctly to make them both visually appealing and easy to understand.

Step-by-Step Guide:

- First, select the chart that you want to format.
- Once the chart is selected, the "Chart Tools" tab should appear at the top of the Excel window. Click on this tab to reveal the "Design" and "Format" sub-tabs.
- Under the "Design" sub-tab, you can choose from a variety of pre-made chart styles, including colors and layouts. Simply click on the desired style to apply it to your chart.
- To customize your chart further, click on the "Format" sub-tab. This will reveal several options for formatting your chart, including the ability to change the chart type, axis labels, and chart title.
- To change the color scheme of your chart, select the chart element that you want to modify (e.g. chart background, chart area, data series, etc.) and then click on the "Fill" or "Border" buttons under the "Format" sub-tab. From here, you can select from a variety of colors, patterns, and gradients.
- To change the font style of your chart's text, select the chart element that you want to modify (e.g. axis labels, chart title, legend, etc.) and then click on the "Font" button under the "Format" sub-tab. From here, you can choose from a variety of font styles, sizes, and colors.
- To add or modify axis labels, simply click on the axis that you want to modify and then select the "Axis Options" button under the "Format" sub-

tab. From here, you can change the label text, font, and position.
- To add or modify the chart title, select the chart title and then click on the "Chart Title" button under the "Format" sub-tab. From here, you can change the title text, font, and position.
- Once you have finished formatting your chart, you can preview your changes by selecting the "Preview" button under the "Format" sub-tab. This will show you how your chart will look before you apply the changes.
- When you are satisfied with your chart formatting, simply click on the "Close" button under the "Format" sub-tab to apply the changes to your chart.

Chart Template

Charts are an essential tool in Excel to visualize data and communicate insights effectively. However, creating a chart from scratch can be time-consuming, especially when you need to use the same style and formatting repeatedly. In this case, using a chart template can save you time and effort by applying a predefined set of formatting and design settings to your chart.

Step-by-Step Guide:

- Select the chart you want to format with a chart template.
- Go to the "Design" tab in the Excel ribbon.
- In the "Type" group, click on the "Change Chart Type" button.
- In the "Change Chart Type" dialog box, click on the "Templates" tab.
- Choose the chart template you want to apply to your chart.
- Click on the "Use Template" button.
- Excel will apply the selected chart template to your chart.
- Customize the chart as necessary, such as changing the chart title, data labels, or axis labels.
- Save your chart as a template to reuse it in the future.
- To save your chart as a template, right-click on the chart and select "Save as Template" from the context menu.
- In the "Save Chart Template" dialog box, enter a name for the template and click "Save."
- Your chart template is now saved and can be accessed from the "Templates" tab in the "Change Chart Type" dialog box.

Chart templates are saved in the default chart template folder. You can change the default chart template folder location by going to the "File" tab, selecting "Options," and then selecting "Save."

Check IF 0 (Zero) Then Blank in Excel

When working with data in Excel, there may be cases where you want to display a blank cell instead of a zero when a certain condition is met. This is where the "IF" function in Excel comes in handy. By using the IF function along with the logical test for zero, you can check if a cell contains a zero and return a blank cell instead.

Step-by-Step Guide:

- Open a new or existing Excel worksheet.
- Enter the data that you want to evaluate.
- Select the cell or cells where you want to apply the check.
- Type the following formula into the formula bar: =IF(A1=0,"",A1)
- This formula checks if the cell A1 contains a zero. If it does, the formula returns a blank cell. If it doesn't, the formula returns the value in cell A1.
- Press Enter to apply the formula to the selected cell or cells.
- The result will display a blank cell where the original value was zero, and the original value where it was not zero.

In the formula above, "A1" is the cell that you want to check for zero. If you are checking a different cell, simply change "A1" to the appropriate cell reference.

Check IF a Value Exists in a Range in Excel

Checking if a value exists in a range is a common task in Excel, and it can be useful in many scenarios. For example, you may want to check if a specific product is available in your inventory, or if a particular customer has already placed an order. By using the IF function with a combination of other Excel functions, you can quickly determine if a value exists in a range and take appropriate actions.

Step-by-Step Guide:

- Simplifying your data analysis tasks by automating the process of finding specific values in a large dataset
- Streamlining your decision-making process by quickly identifying if a specific value is present or not
- Reducing the likelihood of errors in your data analysis by providing a reliable way of checking if a value exists in a range.
- Instructions:

To check if a value exists in a range in Excel, follow these steps:

- Select the cell where you want to display the result of your formula.
- Type the following formula: =IF(COUNTIF(range,value)>0,"Value exists","Value does not exist")
- Replace "range" with the range of cells you want to search for the value.
- Replace "value" with the value you want to search for.
- Press Enter to see the result of the formula.

If the value exists in the range, the formula will return "Value exists". If the value does not exist in the range, the formula will return "Value does not exist".

Check Mark (Excel Shortcut)

The check mark symbol is a commonly used icon in various industries and applications. In Excel, the check mark symbol can be used to indicate completion of a task, approval of a document or project, or simply as a visual aid to highlight important information. The check mark symbol can be inserted into cells using the Wingdings font and the CHAR function.

Step-by-Step Guide:

- Select the cell where you want to insert the check mark symbol.
- Click on the "Insert" tab in the Excel ribbon.
- Click on "Symbol" in the "Text" section.
- In the "Symbol" window, select "Wingdings" from the "Font" drop-down menu.
- Scroll down in the symbol list to find the check mark symbol (it is usually the last symbol in the list).
- Click on the check mark symbol to select it, then click on "Insert" to add it to the cell.
- Alternatively, you can use the Excel shortcut by holding down the "Alt" key and typing "0252" on the numeric keypad (make sure the Num Lock is on).
- Release the "Alt" key, and the check mark symbol should appear in the cell.

If the check mark symbol does not appear, try changing the font to Wingdings 2 or Wingdings 3 and repeat the steps above.

Clear Contents (Excel Shortcut)

Clearing the contents of cells is a common task in Excel. It can help you remove unwanted data or start with a clean slate for new data entry. The Clear Contents Excel shortcut is a quick and efficient way to clear the contents of cells without having to use the mouse.

Step-by-Step Guide:

- Select the cell or range of cells that you want to clear the contents of.
- Press the Delete key on your keyboard.
- If a confirmation dialog box appears, select the "Clear Contents" option.
- The contents of the selected cells should now be cleared.

If you want to delete the entire cell (including any formatting or comments), use the Cut Excel shortcut (Ctrl+X) instead of the Clear Contents shortcut.

Clear Formatting

Clear Formatting is an Excel trick that allows you to remove any formatting applied to a selected cell or range of cells, such as font style, font size, font color, fill color, borders, and more. It is a useful feature that helps to restore the default formatting of cells quickly and easily.

Step-by-Step Guide:

- Select the cell(s) or range of cells from which you want to remove formatting.
- Right-click on the selected cell(s) and choose "Clear Formats" from the context menu. Alternatively, you can click on the "Clear Formats" button in the "Editing" group of the "Home" tab in the ribbon.
- Excel will remove all formatting from the selected cell(s) or range of cells, leaving only the cell value(s) behind.

If you only want to remove specific formatting elements, such as borders or fill color, you can use the "Clear Borders" or "Clear Contents" options from the context menu or ribbon.

Clipboard

Excel's clipboard feature is a powerful tool that allows you to copy and paste data between different worksheets, workbooks, and even applications. The clipboard can store multiple items at once, allowing you to easily switch between them and paste them wherever you need.

Step-by-Step Guide:

- Copy Data: To use the clipboard, start by selecting the data you want to copy. You can do this by clicking and dragging your mouse over the data, or by using the keyboard shortcuts Ctrl + C (Windows) or Command + C (Mac).
- Access the Clipboard: Once you've copied your data, you can access the clipboard by clicking on the Home tab in the Excel ribbon, and then clicking on the Clipboard group. Alternatively, you can use the keyboard shortcut Ctrl + C twice to open the clipboard.
- View Clipboard: The clipboard panel will appear on the left-hand side of your screen, showing the current contents of the clipboard. If you've just copied data, it will appear as the first item in the list.
- Add More Data: If you want to add more data to the clipboard, simply copy it as you normally would. It will be added to the clipboard along with any other items you've copied previously.
- Paste Data: To paste data from the clipboard, place your cursor where you want to paste the data, and then click on the item in the clipboard that you want to paste. You can also use the keyboard shortcut Ctrl + V (Windows) or Command + V (Mac) to paste the data.

- Clear Clipboard: To clear the clipboard, click on the Clear All button in the Clipboard group of the Home tab, or use the keyboard shortcut Ctrl + Alt + A.

Close (Excel Shortcut)

In Excel, the Close shortcut is used to close the current workbook. This shortcut can be useful when you have finished working on a particular Excel file and want to close it quickly without using your mouse.

Step-by-Step Guide:

- Press the "Alt" key on your keyboard.
- While holding down the "Alt" key, press the "F" key.
- Release both keys.
- Press the "C" key.

Alternatively, you can use the following shortcut:

- Press the "Ctrl" key on your keyboard.
- While holding down the "Ctrl" key, press the "W" key.

Combine IF and AND Functions in Excel

The IF function in Excel is used to perform a logical test and return one value for a TRUE result and another value for a FALSE result. The AND function, on the other hand, is used to check if all the conditions in a formula are TRUE. Combining the IF and AND functions can be useful when you want to perform a test that requires multiple conditions to be met. For instance, you might want to test whether a student has passed a test based on achieving a certain score in multiple sections.

Step-by-Step Guide:

- First, select the cell where you want to enter the formula.
- Begin the formula with the IF function, followed by an opening bracket (=IF(.
- Enter the logical test you want to perform within the IF function, using the AND function to combine multiple conditions. The syntax for the AND function is: =AND(logical1, [logical2], ...). You can include as many logical arguments as you need within the AND function.
- After the AND function, enter a comma and the value you want to return if the test is TRUE.
- Enter a comma and the value you want to return if the test is FALSE.
- Close the bracket and press enter to complete the formula.

Combine IF and OR Functions in Excel

The IF and OR functions are two of the most commonly used functions in Excel. They allow you to perform conditional logic on your data, making it easier to analyze and understand. When you combine the IF and OR functions in Excel, you can create even more complex and powerful conditional statements.

The IF function checks whether a condition is true or false, and then returns a value based on the result. The OR function allows you to test multiple conditions at once and returns true if any of the conditions are true. By combining these two functions, you can create a formula that checks for multiple conditions and returns a value based on the result.

Step-by-Step Guide:

- Start by opening a new or existing Excel workbook.
- Select a cell where you want to create your formula.
- Type the following formula: =IF(OR(condition1, condition2), value_if_true, value_if_false)
- Replace "condition1" and "condition2" with the conditions you want to test. You can include as many conditions as you need, separated by commas.
- Replace "value_if_true" with the value you want to return if any of the conditions are true.
- Replace "value_if_false" with the value you want to return if none of the conditions are true.
- Press Enter to apply the formula to the cell.

Compare Two Cells in Excel

Comparing two cells in Excel is a common task when working with data. It allows you to check if the values in two cells are the same or different. This can be useful when checking for errors or inconsistencies in your data. Excel provides several ways to compare two cells, including using simple operators like "=" or "<>", or using more advanced functions like IF and AND.

Step-by-Step Guide:

- Open the Excel worksheet that contains the cells you want to compare.
- Select the cell where you want to display the result of the comparison.
- Enter the comparison formula in the selected cell. The formula should start with an equal sign (=) followed by the comparison operator you want to use, and the two cell references separated by a comma. For example, to check if cell A1 is equal to cell B1, use the following formula: =A1=B1. To check if cell A1 is not equal to cell B1, use the following formula: =A1<>B1.
- Press the Enter key to apply the formula and display the result of the comparison in the selected cell. If the values in the two cells are the same, the formula will return TRUE; otherwise, it will return FALSE.

Using IF Function:

- Open the Excel worksheet that contains the cells you want to compare.
- Select the cell where you want to display the result of the comparison.

- Enter the following formula in the selected cell: =IF(A1=B1,"Match","No match"). This formula uses the IF function to check if the values in cells A1 and B1 are the same. If they are, the formula returns the text "Match"; otherwise, it returns the text "No match". You can customize the text to match your needs.
- Press the Enter key to apply the formula and display the result of the comparison in the selected cell.

Using Conditional Formatting:

- Open the Excel worksheet that contains the cells you want to compare.
- Select the two cells you want to compare.
- Click the Home tab in the Excel ribbon.
- Click the Conditional Formatting button in the Styles group.
- Select "Highlight Cells Rules" from the drop-down menu.
- Select "Equal To" from the sub-menu.
- In the dialog box that appears, enter the reference to the cell you want to compare the selected cells to.
- Click the OK button to apply the conditional formatting. The selected cells will be highlighted if they match the comparison cell.

Compare Two Dates in Excel

In Excel, it's common to compare dates to see if they are equal, greater than, or less than each other. This can be useful in many situations, such as calculating the duration between two dates, comparing project deadlines, or analyzing trends over time. In this guide, you will learn how to compare two dates in Excel using different operators.

Step-by-Step Guide:

- Enter the two dates that you want to compare in separate cells. For example, you can enter one date in cell A1 and the other date in cell B1.
- Select the cell where you want to display the result of the comparison. For example, you can select cell C1.
- To check if the first date is greater than the second date, enter the following formula in cell C1: =IF(A1>B1,"Yes","No"). This formula will compare the two dates and return "Yes" if the first date is greater than the second date, and "No" otherwise.
- To check if the first date is less than the second date, enter the following formula in cell C1: =IF(A1<B1,"Yes","No"). This formula will compare the two dates and return "Yes" if the first date is less than the second date, and "No" otherwise.
- To check if the two dates are equal, enter the following formula in cell C1: =IF(A1=B1,"Yes","No"). This formula will compare the two dates and return "Yes" if they are equal, and "No" otherwise.
- You can also use other operators to compare the two dates, such as greater than or equal to (>=)

and less than or equal to (<=). To check if the first date is greater than or equal to the second date, enter the following formula in cell C1: =IF(A1>=B1,"Yes","No"). This formula will compare the two dates and return "Yes" if the first date is greater than or equal to the second date, and "No" otherwise.

- To check if the first date is less than or equal to the second date, enter the following formula in cell C1: =IF(A1<=B1,"Yes","No"). This formula will compare the two dates and return "Yes" if the first date is less than or equal to the second date, and "No" otherwise.
- Once you have entered the formula in cell C1, press Enter to calculate the result.
- The result will be displayed in cell C1 as either "Yes" or "No", depending on the comparison operator used.
- You can now copy the formula in cell C1 and paste it to other cells if you want to compare other pairs of dates.

When comparing dates in Excel, it's important to make sure that the dates are entered correctly and formatted as dates. If the dates are not formatted correctly, the comparison may not work as expected.

Concatenate with a Line Break in Excel

Concatenation is a common task in Excel where you combine the contents of two or more cells into a single cell. However, sometimes you may want to add a line break or a new line between the contents of the cells. This is useful when you want to display the contents in separate lines or paragraphs.

Step-by-Step Guide:

- Open Microsoft Excel and create a new blank workbook.
- Type the text or values that you want to concatenate in separate cells. For example, we will use cells A1 and A2 and concatenate their contents with a line break.
- Select the cell where you want to display the concatenated text. For example, we will select cell A3.
- Type the following formula in the formula bar:
- =CONCATENATE(A1, CHAR(10), A2)
- The CHAR(10) function inserts a line break or a new line character in the text string. You can also use the formula =A1 & CHAR(10) & A2 to achieve the same result.
- Press the Enter key to execute the formula. The contents of cells A1 and A2 will be concatenated with a line break and displayed in cell A3.
- Format the cell A3 as "Wrap Text" to ensure that the concatenated text is displayed in separate lines.

Conditional Ranking in Excel using SUMPRODUCT Function [RANKIF]

Conditional ranking is an important feature of Excel that helps users to rank data based on a certain condition or criteria. The SUMPRODUCT function in Excel can be used to perform conditional ranking, commonly known as RANKIF. This function can be used to find out the rank of a value in a data set based on a specified condition.

Step-by-Step Guide:

- First, arrange the data set in a tabular form with each column having a unique header.
- Select an empty cell where you want to display the rank of a specific value based on a condition.
- Type the following formula into the selected cell:
- sql
- Copy code
- =RANK(IF(range=criteria,1,0),IF(range=criteria,range,""))
- Replace "range" with the column range that contains the data to be ranked.
- Replace "criteria" with the condition or criteria based on which you want to rank the data.
- Press Enter to apply the formula to the cell.
- The result will show the rank of the value based on the specified condition.

If there are ties in the data, then the same rank will be given to those items. For example, if two employees have the same sales, then both will be assigned the same rank, and the next rank will be skipped.

Convert Date to Number in Excel

In Excel, dates are typically stored as serial numbers, with each date assigned a unique number. While this can be useful for some calculations, there may be times when you need to convert a date to a number for other purposes. For example, you may need to use the number to perform a mathematical calculation or use it to sort or filter data based on dates.

Step-by-Step Guide:

- Open your Excel spreadsheet and select the cell containing the date you want to convert.
- In a blank cell, enter the formula =VALUE(cell reference), replacing "cell reference" with the reference of the cell containing the date you want to convert. For example, if the date is in cell A1, the formula would be =VALUE(A1).
- Press Enter on your keyboard to apply the formula.
- The date will now be converted to a number, which you can see in the formula bar.
- If you want to format the number as a date, you can right-click on the cell and select "Format Cells." In the Format Cells dialog box, select "Date" and choose the desired format.
- When you convert a date to a number, Excel uses the same serial number system as described earlier, with January 1, 1900 being assigned the number 1. So, if you convert January 1, 2023 to a number, it will be 44435 (assuming the default date format).

Count Between Two Numbers (COUNTIFS) in Excel

In Excel, there are several built-in functions to count data based on specific criteria. One such function is the COUNTIFS function, which allows you to count the number of cells that meet multiple conditions. The COUNTIFS function is especially useful when you want to count cells that fall within a certain range of values. By using the COUNTIFS function, you can easily count cells that meet two or more criteria, including cells that fall between two numbers.

Step-by-Step Guide:

- Open your Excel workbook and select the cell where you want to display the count result.
- Type the following formula into the formula bar: =COUNTIFS(range1,">"&lower_value, range2,"<"&upper_value), where:
- range1 is the range of cells you want to count
- lower_value is the lower number of the range you want to count
- range2 is the same range as range1
- upper_value is the upper number of the range you want to count
- Replace "range1", "range2", "lower_value", and "upper_value" with the appropriate cell ranges and values for your data.
- Press Enter to complete the formula.
- The cell you selected in step 1 will now display the number of cells that meet the criteria of falling between the two specified values.
- Make sure that you use the correct syntax when typing the formula. The greater than (>) and less

than (<) signs must be enclosed in quotation marks and preceded by an ampersand (&).

Count Blank (Empty) Cells using COUNTIF in Excel

In Excel, it's often necessary to count the number of blank or empty cells in a range of data. This can be useful for a variety of reasons, such as identifying incomplete data or tracking the progress of data entry. The COUNTIF function can be used to accomplish this task by counting the number of cells in a range that meet a specific criteria, in this case being blank.

Step-by-Step Guide:

- Select the cell where you want the count of blank cells to appear.
- Type "=COUNTBLANK(" into the formula bar without the quotes.
- Select the range of cells you want to count the blank cells from.
- Type ")" and press Enter.
- You can also directly specify the range in the COUNTBLANK function, such as "=COUNTBLANK(A1:A10)" to count the blank cells in the range A1 to A10.

Count Cells Less than a Particular Value (COUNTIF) in Excel

Counting the number of cells that contain a specific value or meet a certain condition is a common task in Excel. The COUNTIF function in Excel is a powerful tool that allows you to count the number of cells that meet a certain criteria.

Step-by-Step Guide:

- Open a new or existing Excel worksheet and select the cell where you want to display the count result.
- Type the equal sign (=) to begin the formula.
- Type "COUNTIF(" to begin the COUNTIF function.
- Select the range of cells that you want to count. This is the range where the values will be compared to the criteria.
- Type a comma (,) to separate the range argument from the criteria argument.
- Type the criteria for the cells you want to count. In this case, you want to count cells that are less than a particular value, so type "<" followed by the value. For example, if you want to count cells less than 50, you would type "<50".
- Close the parentheses to complete the COUNTIF function.
- Press the Enter key to display the result.

Count Cells Not Equal To in Excel (COUNTIF)

Counting cells based on a specific criterion is a common task in Excel. One of the most useful functions to achieve this is the COUNTIF function. It counts the number of cells in a range that meet a certain condition. However, sometimes we need to count the number of cells that do not meet a certain condition. In such cases, we can use the COUNTIF function with the "not equal to" operator "<>".

Step-by-Step Guide:

- Open a new or existing Excel worksheet.
- Select the cell where you want to display the result of the count function.
- Type the formula "=COUNTIF(range,"<>value")" in the formula bar, where "range" is the range of cells you want to count and "value" is the value or condition you want to exclude from the count.
- Press "Enter" to execute the formula and display the result.
- For example, if you want to count the number of cells in the range A1:A10 that are not equal to the value "0", the formula would be "=COUNTIF(A1:A10,"<>0")".

Note that you can use any value or condition you want to exclude from the count, such as a text string, a number, or a logical expression. Also, you can use multiple criteria by separating them with the "&" operator. For example, if you want to count the number of cells in the range A1:A10 that are not equal to the value "0" or the value "1", the formula would be "=COUNTIF(A1:A10,"<>0"&"<>1")".

Count Cells That Are Not Blank in Excel

When working with data in Excel, it is often necessary to count the number of cells that are not blank in a particular range. This can be useful when analyzing data or preparing reports. The COUNTA function in Excel can be used to count non-blank cells in a range.

Step-by-Step Guide:

- Open the Excel worksheet that contains the data you want to count.
- Select the cell where you want to display the count.
- Type the equal sign "=" to start the formula.
- Type "COUNTA(" (without the quotes).
- Select the range of cells you want to count.
- Type ")" (without the quotes) to close the formula.
- Press Enter.

Count Cells with Text in Excel

In Excel, there are times when you need to count the number of cells that contain text. This could be useful, for example, when you want to find out how many cells in a range of data contain specific words or phrases. The COUNTIF function in Excel can be used to achieve this.

Step-by-Step Guide:

- Open the Excel sheet and select the cell where you want to display the result.
- Enter the formula =COUNTIF(range,"*") in the cell, where "range" is the range of cells you want to count.
- Press the Enter key on your keyboard. The result will be displayed in the selected cell.

In the formula, the asterisk (*) is used as a wildcard character that matches any number of characters in the cell. So, the formula will count all the cells in the range that contain any amount of text.

Count Greater Than 0 (COUNTIF) in Excel

Counting the number of cells that meet a certain criteria is a common task in Excel. One useful criteria is to count the number of cells that have a value greater than zero. This can be helpful when working with financial data or any data that includes positive values. By using the COUNTIF function in Excel, we can easily count the number of cells that meet this criteria.

Step-by-Step Guide:

- Open a new or existing Excel spreadsheet.
- Enter your data into a range of cells in the spreadsheet.
- Decide on a cell where you would like to display the count result.
- Select the cell where you would like to display the count result.
- Type the following formula into the selected cell: =COUNTIF(range,">0")
- Replace "range" in the formula with the range of cells that you want to count.
- Press the Enter key on your keyboard to calculate the formula.
- The selected cell should now display the number of cells in the specified range that have a value greater than zero.

If you want to count cells that are greater than or equal to zero, you can modify the formula to say ">=0" instead of ">0".

Count Specific Characters in Excel

Excel is a powerful tool that can be used to analyze and manipulate large sets of data. One common task is to count the number of cells in a range that contain a specific character or set of characters. This can be useful for various applications, such as counting the number of cells that contain a certain keyword in a list of emails or analyzing the frequency of certain characters in a dataset.

Step-by-Step Guide:

- Open Excel and create a new worksheet.
- In the worksheet, enter the data that you want to analyze. For example, let's say you want to count the number of cells that contain the letter "a" in a range of cells from A1 to A10.
- Click on the cell where you want to display the result of the count function.
- Type "=COUNTIF(A1:A10,"a")" into the cell (without the quotation marks).
- Press Enter to display the result of the count function.

The COUNTIF function in Excel allows users to count the number of cells in a range that meet specific criteria. In this case, we are using the "*" wildcard character to match any text before or after the letter "a" in the cells we want to count. This allows us to count cells that contain the letter "a" anywhere in the cell, not just cells that begin with or end with "a".

By following these simple steps, users can easily count the number of cells in a range that contain specific characters. This allows for quick and efficient analysis of large datasets, making it a valuable tool for data analysis, research, and reporting.

Count the Total Number of Cells from a Range in Excel

Counting the total number of cells in a range is a basic function that is frequently used in Excel. The COUNT function in Excel is a simple way to count the total number of cells in a range. This function can be used to count the number of cells in a single row, column, or in multiple rows and columns.

Step-by-Step Guide:

- Open an Excel workbook and enter your data in a range of cells.
- Select the cell where you want to display the total number of cells from the range.
- Type the following formula: =COUNT(range), where 'range' is the range of cells that you want to count.

Count Unique Values in a Pivot Table in Excel

Pivot tables in Excel are a powerful tool for analyzing and summarizing large data sets. One common task is to count the number of unique values within a pivot table. This can be useful in identifying the number of unique items, customers, or any other category within a dataset.

Step-by-Step Guide:

- Select the data set you want to use for the pivot table.
- Click on the "Insert" tab and select "Pivot Table" from the "Tables" group.
- In the "Create PivotTable" dialog box, select the range of cells that contains your data set.
- Choose where you want to place the pivot table (e.g. a new worksheet or an existing worksheet).
- Drag the field that contains the values you want to count to the "Values" area of the PivotTable Fields pane.
- The field will be automatically set to sum the values. To change this, click on the drop-down arrow next to the field name and select "Value Field Settings".
- In the "Value Field Settings" dialog box, select "Count" under the "Summarize value field by" section.
- Click "OK" to close the dialog box.
- Drag the field that contains the unique values you want to count to the "Rows" area of the PivotTable Fields pane.
- The pivot table will now display the count of unique values for each item in the selected field.

If you have multiple fields in the "Rows" area, you can use the "Value Field Settings" dialog box to count unique values for each item in the selected fields.

COUNT Vs. COUNTA

When working with data in Excel, it is common to use functions to perform calculations on that data. Two such functions are COUNT and COUNTA. While both of these functions count the number of cells in a range, there is an important difference between them.

COUNT function counts only cells that contain numbers, whereas COUNTA counts all cells that are not blank. This means that COUNT will only count cells that contain numeric values, while COUNTA will count cells that contain any type of data, including text, dates, and blank cells.

Step-by-Step Guide:

- Select the range of cells that you want to count.
- To use the COUNT function, enter the following formula in a cell: =COUNT(range)
- Replace "range" with the range of cells that you want to count.
- This will return the count of cells that contain numbers.
- To use the COUNTA function, enter the following formula in a cell: =COUNTA(range)
- Replace "range" with the range of cells that you want to count.
- This will return the count of cells that are not blank, including cells that contain text and other non-numeric data.
- Use the results of these functions in further calculations or analysis as needed.

Remember that COUNT and COUNTA are just two of many functions available in Excel for working with data.

Understanding the differences between them and when to use each one is a key step towards accurate and efficient data analysis.

Count Words

Counting words is an essential operation when working with large text documents or in situations where word count matters, such as academic writing, content creation, or translation. Excel provides a built-in function that enables you to count the number of words in a cell or range of cells quickly.

Step-by-Step Guide:

- Open an Excel worksheet and enter the text in the cell(s) you want to count.
- Click on an empty cell where you want to display the word count result.
- In the formula bar, type "=SUMPRODUCT(--(LEN(A1:A10)>0),LEN(TRIM(A1:A10))-LEN(SUBSTITUTE(A1:A10," ",""))+1)" and press enter.
- Replace A1:A10 with the range of cells you want to count words.
- The cell you selected in step 2 will display the word count of the range you specified.

Explanation of the Formula:

- LEN(A1:A10)>0: checks if the cell is not empty.
- TRIM(A1:A10): removes any leading or trailing spaces in the cell's text.
- SUBSTITUTE(A1:A10," ",""): replaces all spaces with empty strings to count the number of spaces in the cell's text.
- LEN(TRIM(A1:A10))-LEN(SUBSTITUTE(A1:A10," ",""))+1: calculates the number of words in the cell.

This formula is case-sensitive, meaning it will count "Hello" and "hello" as two separate words.

Count Years Between Two Dates in Excel

Counting the number of years between two dates can be useful in various applications, such as calculating the age of a person, determining the length of a project, or finding the duration of an investment. Excel provides a simple formula to count the number of years between two dates.

Step-by-Step Guide:

- Open Excel and create a new workbook.
- Enter the start date in cell A1 and the end date in cell B1. You can use any date format as per your requirement.
- In cell C1, enter the following formula:
  =DATEDIF(A1,B1,"y")
- Press Enter. The result will be displayed in cell C1, which represents the number of years between the two dates.
- The third argument in the DATEDIF function, "y", specifies that we want to calculate the difference in years. If you want to calculate the difference in months, you can use "m" instead of "y" in the formula. Similarly, for calculating the difference in days, use "d".
- If you want to include the end date in the calculation, you can use the following formula instead:
  =DATEDIF(A1,B1+1,"y")
- Press Enter. The result will be displayed in cell C1, which represents the number of years between the two dates, including the end date.

Create a Bullet Chart in Excel

A bullet chart is a data visualization tool that displays a single measure or metric against a qualitative scale with visual cues to indicate performance. It is commonly used to show progress towards goals, as well as to compare actual and target values. The bullet chart is similar to a bar chart but offers greater efficiency and clarity in communicating information.

Step-by-Step Guide:

- Enter your data: In the first column, enter the category or measure name. In the second column, enter the actual value. In the third column, enter the target value.
- Select the data: Click and drag to select the data you want to use in your bullet chart.
- Insert a new chart: Click on the Insert tab on the Ribbon and select the Stacked Bar Chart from the Charts section. Choose the first option under 2-D Stacked Bar Chart.
- Remove unnecessary elements: Right-click on the chart and select "Select Data". In the "Legend Entries (Series)" section, click on the "Edit" button for the "Target Value" series and change the "Series overlap" to 100%. Remove the "Legend Key" for the "Actual Value" series.
- Adjust the axis: Right-click on the horizontal axis and select "Format Axis". In the "Axis Options" section, set the "Minimum" to the minimum value of the data and the "Maximum" to the maximum value of the data. Uncheck the box for "Values in reverse order". Set the "Major tick mark type" to "None" and the "Minor tick mark type" to "None".

- Add reference lines: Right-click on the chart and select "Add Data Labels". Click on the "Data Labels" and select "Value from Cells". Select the range of the target values and click "OK". Right-click on any of the target data labels and select "Format Data Labels". In the "Label Options" section, check the box for "Value". In the "Label Position" section, select "Below". In the "Number" section, select "Custom" and enter "0" for the "Decimal places". Click "Close". Right-click on the target data labels again and select "Format Data Labels". In the "Fill & Line" section, select "No Fill". Click "Close". This will add a horizontal line to the chart that represents the target value.
- Add color to the chart: Right-click on the actual bar in the chart and select "Format Data Series". In the "Fill & Line" section, select a color for the bar that represents the actual value. Click "Close".
- Customize the chart: Format the chart as desired by changing the font size, color, chart title, and other elements.

Create a Data Validation with Date Range

Data validation is an important feature in Excel that allows you to control what data can be entered into a cell or range of cells. By using data validation, you can set up rules to ensure that the data entered in a cell meets specific criteria. One of the most useful applications of data validation is to restrict input to a specific date range. This ensures that users only enter dates within a specified range and helps to maintain the integrity of the data.

Step-by-Step Guide:

- Open your Excel worksheet and select the cell or range of cells where you want to apply the data validation.
- Click on the "Data" tab in the ribbon.
- Click on the "Data Validation" button in the "Data Tools" group.
- In the "Data Validation" dialog box, select "Date" from the "Allow" drop-down list.
- In the "Start date" and "End date" fields, enter the start and end dates for the date range you want to allow.
- In the "Data" tab, you can choose to show an input message or an error message if the entered date is outside the specified range. To display an input message, check the "Show input message when cell is selected" box and enter the message you want to display in the "Input message" tab. To display an error message, check the "Show error alert after invalid data is entered" box and enter the message you want to display in the "Error message" tab.
- Click "OK" to apply the data validation to the selected cell or range of cells.

Now, whenever a user tries to enter a date outside of the specified range, Excel will display an error message or input message (depending on your settings) to alert the user that the data entered is invalid. By following these simple steps, you can easily create a data validation with a date range in Excel.

Create a Dynamic Chart Range in Excel

Creating a dynamic chart range in Excel allows you to automatically update your chart's data range as new data is added or removed. This can save you time and effort when creating and updating charts, especially if your data changes frequently.

Step-by-Step Guide:

- Select the data you want to use in your chart, including the headers.
- On the ribbon, click on the "Formulas" tab.
- Click on "Define Name" in the "Defined Names" section.
- In the "New Name" dialog box, enter a name for your dynamic range, such as "ChartData".
- In the "Refers to" box, enter the formula that defines your data range. For example, if your data is in cells A1:B10, you can enter "=Sheet1!$A$1:INDEX(Sheet1!$B:$10,COUNTA(Sheet1!$B:$10))". This formula will automatically adjust the range based on the number of non-blank cells in column B.
- Click "OK" to save your new name.
- Create your chart by selecting the data range and choosing your chart type.
- Right-click on your chart and select "Select Data".
- In the "Select Data Source" dialog box, click on "Edit" under "Legend Entries (Series)".
- In the "Series Values" box, enter the name you gave your dynamic range, preceded by the worksheet name and an exclamation point. For example, if your dynamic range is named "ChartData" and your data is in Sheet1, enter "Sheet1!ChartData".

- Click "OK" to close the dialog box and update your chart.

Create a HEAT MAP in Excel (Simple Steps) + Template

A heat map is a type of data visualization that displays data values in a table or matrix format using colors. Heat maps are useful for displaying large amounts of data and making it easier to interpret the data quickly. In Excel, you can easily create a heat map using conditional formatting.

Step-by-Step Guide:

- Open a new or existing Excel workbook.
- Select the range of cells that you want to use for your heat map.
- Click on the Home tab, then click on Conditional Formatting, and select Color Scales.
- Choose the color scale that you want to use for your heat map.
- Adjust the minimum and maximum values to fit the range of data you want to visualize.
- Click OK to apply the heat map to your selected range.

Creating a Heat Map Using a Template:

- Download a heat map template from a reliable source.
- Open the downloaded template in Excel.
- Replace the sample data with your own data.
- Adjust the color scale and other settings as needed.
- Save your completed heat map.

Create a HISTOGRAM in Excel

A histogram is a graphical representation of data distribution. It shows how many values fall into specific ranges, or bins, and how many values fall into each bin. Histograms are useful in analyzing large data sets and identifying patterns and trends in the data. They are commonly used in statistics, finance, and scientific research.

Step-by-Step Guide:

- Open Microsoft Excel and create a new spreadsheet.
- Enter your data into a column in the spreadsheet.
- Select the cell where you want to create the histogram.
- Click on the "Insert" tab at the top of the screen.
- In the "Charts" group, click on "Histogram" and select the type of histogram you want to create.
- Excel will automatically generate a histogram based on your data. You can then customize the histogram by adjusting the bin size, the axis labels, and the chart style.
- To adjust the bin size, right-click on the horizontal axis and select "Format Axis". Under "Axis Options", select "Bin Width" and enter the bin size you want to use.
- To adjust the axis labels, right-click on the horizontal or vertical axis and select "Format Axis". Under "Axis Options", you can change the axis label range, the label interval, and other formatting options.
- To change the chart style, click on the chart and select "Chart Design" in the ribbon at the top of the screen. Here you can choose from a variety of different styles and formats.

Template:

If you prefer to use a pre-designed template for your histogram, Excel has several built-in templates that you can use.

To access these templates, follow these steps:

- Click on the "File" tab at the top of the screen.
- Select "New" from the left-hand menu.
- In the search bar, type "histogram" and press enter.
- Excel will show you a list of available histogram templates. Select the template you want to use and click "Create".
- Excel will generate a new spreadsheet with the template already applied. You can then enter your data into the template and customize it as needed.

Create a Horizontal Filter in Excel

Excel provides a number of filtering options to help users analyze and organize their data. One of these options is the horizontal filter, which allows users to filter their data by row instead of by column. This can be particularly useful when working with large datasets, as it allows users to quickly identify and isolate specific rows of data.

Step-by-Step Guide:

- Open the Excel workbook containing the data you want to filter.
- Select the row that you want to use as the filter criteria.
- Go to the "Data" tab in the Excel ribbon.
- Click on the "Filter" button.
- Click on the filter arrow next to the column you want to filter by.
- In the dropdown menu, select "Filter by Selected Cell's Value".
- In the "Filter by Selected Cell's Value" dialog box, select "Equals" and then type in the value that you want to filter by.
- Click "OK" to apply the filter.
- Repeat steps 5-8 for each additional column you want to filter by.
- To remove the filter, simply click on the "Clear" button in the "Sort & Filter" group on the "Data" tab.

You can also use the "Custom Filter" option in the filter dialog box to apply more advanced filtering criteria, such as filtering by dates or text strings.

Create a Milestone Chart in Excel

A milestone chart is a useful way to track important events or milestones in a project or process. It helps to visualize the progress of the project and identify any delays or issues that may arise. In Excel, a milestone chart is created using a stacked bar chart with dates and milestones.

Step-by-Step Guide:

- Enter your project data into Excel. You will need to have a list of milestones with their corresponding dates.
- Select the milestone data and insert a stacked bar chart.
- Right-click on the chart and select "Select Data".
- Click on "Add" under the "Legend Entries (Series)" section.
- In the "Edit Series" window, enter the milestone name in the "Series Name" field.
- For the "Series Values", select the range of cells that contain the milestone data.
- Click "OK" to close the "Edit Series" window.
- Repeat steps 4-7 for each milestone.
- Right-click on the horizontal axis and select "Format Axis".
- Under "Axis Options", change the "Axis Type" to "Date Axis".
- Adjust the date range if necessary.
- Right-click on each milestone bar and select "Format Data Series".
- Under "Fill", select "No Fill".
- Under "Border", select a color for the milestone bar border.
- Adjust the border width if necessary.

- Add any additional formatting, such as chart title and legend, as desired.

Using a milestone chart in Excel can help you to easily track the progress of your project and identify any delays or issues. By following these steps, you can create a visually appealing and informative milestone chart to communicate your project's progress with stakeholders and team members.

Create a Pivot Table from Multiple Worksheets

A Pivot Table is a powerful tool in Excel that allows you to summarize and analyze large amounts of data. It can quickly transform raw data into useful information, making it easier to make informed decisions. When working with data spread across multiple worksheets, you can use the Pivot Table to combine the data and summarize it in a single table.

Step-by-Step Guide:

- Open a new worksheet and click on the "PivotTable" button in the "Tables" group on the "Insert" tab.
- In the "Create PivotTable" dialog box, select "Use an external data source" and click "Choose Connection."
- In the "Existing Connections" dialog box, click on the "Browse for More" button and navigate to the folder that contains the worksheets you want to include in the Pivot Table.
- Select the first worksheet you want to include and click "Open."
- In the "Import Data" dialog box, select "PivotTable Report" and click "OK."
- Repeat steps 4 and 5 for each worksheet you want to include in the Pivot Table.
- In the "Create PivotTable" dialog box, select the range of cells containing the data you want to include in the Pivot Table.
- Click "OK" to create the Pivot Table.
- In the "PivotTable Fields" pane, drag and drop the fields you want to include in the Pivot Table into the "Row Labels," "Column Labels," and "Values" areas.

- Customize the Pivot Table as needed by adding filters, sorting, and formatting.

Create a Population Pyramid Chart in Excel

A Population Pyramid Chart, also known as age-sex pyramid, is a graphical representation of the distribution of a population by age group and sex. It is a useful tool for visualizing and comparing the age and sex structure of different populations. In Excel, you can create a Population Pyramid Chart using a combination of bar charts and data series formatting.

Step-by-Step Guide:

- Enter your data : Enter your population data in an Excel spreadsheet. Create two columns, one for age groups and one for the number of people in each age group. It is recommended to have a separate column for males and females.
- Create a bar chart : Select the data range and create a stacked bar chart. To do this, click on the Insert tab in the ribbon, select the Stacked Bar Chart option, and choose the appropriate chart type.
- Format the chart : Right-click on the chart and select Format Chart Area. In the Format Chart Area pane, set the chart area to have no fill, no border, and no shadow.
- Change the data series order : Click on the chart to select it, and then click on the Chart Design tab in the ribbon. Click on the Switch Row/Column button to switch the data series from horizontal to vertical.
- Format the data series : Click on the male data series in the chart to select it, and then right-click and choose Format Data Series. In the Format Data Series pane, change the Series Overlap to 100% and the Gap Width to 0%. Repeat this step for the female data series.

- Add labels : Add axis labels for the age groups and the number of people in each group. You can also add a chart title and data source labels.
- Adjust the chart scale : Adjust the chart scale by right-clicking on the vertical axis and choosing Format Axis. In the Format Axis pane, set the Minimum and Maximum values to the same negative number (e.g. -100) to center the chart. Adjust the major unit to ensure that each age group is evenly spaced.
- Final touches : Add any final touches to the chart, such as adjusting the font size and color, and hiding the legend if desired.

Create a Star Rating Template in Excel

A star rating is a simple yet effective way to rate products or services. It consists of a series of stars, with a higher number of stars indicating a better rating. In Excel, you can create a star rating template to easily rate items, such as products or services, by simply clicking on the stars.

Step-by-Step Guide:

- Open a new workbook in Excel.
- In the first row, create a column for the name of the item being rated, and then create columns for each star rating. For example, if you want to have a 5-star rating system, create 6 columns - one for the name of the item, and one for each star rating (1 star, 2 stars, 3 stars, 4 stars, and 5 stars).
- In the first row of the star rating columns, insert a star symbol into each cell. You can find the star symbol in the "Symbol" section of the "Insert" tab in the ribbon.
- Select the entire row of star ratings, and then right-click and select "Format Cells".
- In the "Format Cells" dialog box, select the "Custom" category and then enter the following custom format code: [>=1]"★";[>=0.5]"☆";" "
- Click "OK" to apply the custom format to the selected cells. This will display a filled star symbol for ratings of 1 or more, a half-filled star symbol for ratings between 0.5 and 1, and a blank space for ratings less than 0.5.
- To rate an item, simply click on the appropriate star rating cell for that item, and the star symbol will automatically fill in based on the custom format.

Create a Step Chart in Excel

A Step Chart is a type of line chart that represents data with discrete steps instead of a continuous line. It is useful in visualizing data that changes at irregular intervals, such as stock market data or sales figures. Step charts make it easy to identify trends in data and can help you make better-informed decisions. In this guide, we will walk through the step-by-step process of creating a step chart in Excel.

Step-by-Step Guide:

- Open a new or existing Excel worksheet and input your data into two columns. The first column should contain the x-axis values, and the second column should contain the y-axis values.
- Select the entire range of data, including both columns.
- Click on the "Insert" tab in the top menu.
- Click on the "Line" chart type.
- Select the "Step Chart" subtype from the list of options.
- Excel will create a default step chart. You can customize the chart by adding axis titles, changing the chart style, or adjusting the color scheme.
- To add axis titles, click on the chart to activate the "Chart Tools" menu.
- Click on the "Layout" tab in the top menu.
- Click on "Axis Titles" and select "Primary Horizontal Axis Title" and "Primary Vertical Axis Title."
- Type in the axis titles in the text boxes that appear.
- To change the chart style, click on the chart to activate the "Chart Tools" menu.
- Click on the "Design" tab in the top menu.

- Select a new chart style from the "Chart Styles" gallery.
- To adjust the color scheme, click on the chart to activate the "Chart Tools" menu.
- Click on the "Format" tab in the top menu.
- Select "Shape Fill" or "Shape Outline" to change the color of the chart elements.
- Your step chart is now complete.

Create a Tornado Chart in Excel

A Tornado Chart is a type of chart that is used to compare the relative importance of different variables or factors. It is also known as a butterfly chart, due to its shape resembling that of a tornado or butterfly. This chart is useful for highlighting the positive and negative aspects of a group of data in a single chart. A Tornado chart is typically used in sensitivity analysis or risk management, to compare the impact of different variables on a particular outcome.

Step-by-Step Guide:

- Prepare the Data : Prepare a table with the data that you want to use in the Tornado chart. The table should have two columns, one for the variables and the other for their corresponding values. In this example, we will be using a table that compares the cost of different components of a product.
- Sort the Data : Sort the data in descending order based on their values. This will ensure that the most significant variables appear at the top of the chart.
- Create a Bar Chart : Create a standard bar chart using the sorted data.
- Flip the Chart: Flip the chart vertically so that the bars appear on the horizontal axis.
- Add a Secondary Axis : Add a secondary axis to the chart, which will allow us to create the tornado chart.
- Format the Chart : Format the chart to make it more visually appealing. You can change the colors, add labels, and adjust the axis scales as needed.

- Create the Tornado Chart : To create the Tornado chart, select the bars representing the negative values and change their fill color to red. Similarly, select the bars representing the positive values and change their fill color to green.
- Finalize the Chart : Finalize the chart by adding a title and any additional labels or formatting that you want.

Create a Yes – No Drop Down in Excel

Drop-down lists in Excel are a useful tool for data entry and analysis. They allow you to select from a pre-defined set of options, which can improve accuracy and speed up the process. A Yes-No drop-down list is a type of drop-down list that only contains two options: "Yes" and "No".

Step-by-Step Guide:

- Open Excel and create a new workbook.
- Enter the data that you want to use for the drop-down list. For example, in cell A1, enter "Yes", and in cell A2, enter "No".
- Select the cell where you want to create the drop-down list. For example, if you want the drop-down list to be in cell B1, select that cell.
- Click on the "Data" tab in the ribbon at the top of the Excel window.
- Click on "Data Validation" in the "Data Tools" group.
- In the "Data Validation" dialog box, make sure that the "Settings" tab is selected.
- In the "Allow" drop-down list, select "List".
- In the "Source" field, enter the range of cells that contain the data for the drop-down list. For example, if the data is in cells A1 and A2, enter "=$A$1:$A$2".
- Make sure that the "In-cell dropdown" option is checked.
- Click on "OK" to close the dialog box and create the drop-down list.
- Test the drop-down list by selecting a cell in the same row as the drop-down list and clicking on the drop-down arrow. You should see the "Yes" and "No" options that you entered earlier.

- If you want to change the options in the drop-down list, simply edit the data in the cells that you specified in the "Source" field. The drop-down list will automatically update to reflect the changes.

Create Interactive Charts in Excel

Excel is a powerful tool for data analysis and visualization. With interactive charts, you can create dynamic and engaging visualizations that allow users to interact with the data and explore different scenarios. Interactive charts are especially useful when presenting data to others or when you need to analyze data yourself in a more engaging way.

Step-by-Step Guide:

- Choose the data that you want to use for the chart.
- Select the data and go to the "Insert" tab on the Excel ribbon.
- Click on the chart type that you want to use for your data.
- Right-click on the chart and select "Select Data" from the menu.
- Click on the "Add" button to add a new series to the chart.
- Select the data range for the new series and give it a name.
- Click OK to close the "Select Data" dialog box.
- Right-click on the chart and select "Format Chart Area" from the menu.
- In the "Format Chart Area" pane, click on the "Fill & Line" tab.
- Choose a color and transparency level for the chart background.
- Click on the "Chart Title" option in the "Format Chart Area" pane.
- Enter a title for the chart.
- Right-click on the chart and select "Add Data Labels" from the menu.
- Click on the "Layout" tab on the Excel ribbon.

- Click on the "Chart Title" button and select "Above Chart" from the drop-down menu.
- Click on the "Legend" button and select "Right" from the drop-down menu.
- Click on the "Data Labels" button and select "Center" from the drop-down menu.
- Save the chart and test the interactivity by selecting different options or parameters.

Create Pivot Chart in Excel

Excel Pivot Charts are visual representations of the data summarized in a PivotTable. They allow you to explore and analyze large datasets in an interactive way. With a pivot chart, you can easily filter, sort, and group data to discover insights and trends. The chart is automatically updated as you make changes to the underlying data in the PivotTable.

Step-by-Step Guide:

- Start by creating a PivotTable in Excel. Select the data you want to summarize and click on the "PivotTable" button in the "Tables" group on the "Insert" tab.
- In the "Create PivotTable" dialog box, make sure that "New Worksheet" is selected and click "OK". This will create a new worksheet where you can build your PivotTable.
- In the "PivotTable Fields" pane, drag the fields you want to use for your chart to the "Values" area. You can also drag fields to the "Rows" and "Columns" areas to group and filter your data.
- Once you have arranged your fields, click anywhere within the PivotTable and go to the "Insert" tab. Click on the "PivotChart" button in the "Charts" group.
- In the "Insert Chart" dialog box, select the type of chart you want to create, such as a column chart or a line chart. You can also choose to create a PivotChart with a PivotTable or a separate PivotChart.
- Once you have selected your chart type, click "OK". Excel will create a new chart based on your PivotTable data.

- Customize your chart as desired by using the "Chart Design" and "Format" tabs on the Ribbon. You can change the chart title, axis labels, colors, and more.
- To interact with your Pivot Chart, use the filtering options available in the PivotTable Fields pane. You can filter data by selecting values from the drop-down lists or by dragging fields to the "Report Filter" area.
- You can also update the data in your PivotTable by editing the source data or by refreshing the PivotTable. The chart will automatically update to reflect any changes you make.

Create WAFFLE CHART in Excel

A waffle chart is a type of visual representation that resembles a square grid, where each square represents a percentage or a fraction of a whole. It is used to show the proportion of different categories within a dataset. Waffle charts are helpful when the categories are not too many, and it is essential to represent them in a simple and visually appealing way.

Step-by-Step Guide:

- Prepare your data: You will need a table with two columns: one for the categories you want to represent and one for their corresponding values. Ensure that the values add up to 100%.
- Insert a square shape: Select the "Insert" tab, click on the "Shapes" button, and choose a square shape. Draw the shape on the worksheet, and adjust its size to your liking.
- Adjust the square's properties: Right-click on the square, select "Format Shape," and choose the "Fill" option. Then, click on the "Solid fill" button and select a color for the square. Under the "Line" option, choose "No line" to remove the border of the square.
- Create a grid: Copy the square shape and paste it several times to create a grid of squares that corresponds to the number of categories you want to represent. Arrange the squares in a grid pattern.
- Calculate the number of squares per category: Multiply each category's percentage by the total number of squares in the grid to get the number of squares that represent each category.
- Fill in the squares: Color the number of squares calculated in step 5 for each category. You can use

different colors or shades of the same color to distinguish between the categories.
- Add a legend: Insert a text box, and type in the category names and their corresponding percentages or values. Adjust the font, size, and position of the legend to your preference.

Currency Format (Excel Shortcut)

Currency formatting is one of the most commonly used formatting options in Excel. It is essential for financial analysis, budgeting, and accounting purposes. Currency formatting allows you to display numbers in a specific currency format, such as dollars, euros, yen, etc. This formatting helps to enhance the readability and professionalism of your financial reports.

Step-by-Step Guide:

- Select the cell or range of cells that you want to format.
- Press the shortcut key combination "Ctrl+Shift+4" (for Windows) or "Command+Shift+4" (for Mac). This shortcut applies the default currency format to the selected cells.
- If you want to change the currency symbol or the number of decimal places, right-click on the cell or range of cells, and select "Format Cells".
- In the "Format Cells" dialog box, click on the "Number" tab.
- In the "Category" list, select "Currency".
- In the "Symbol" list, select the currency symbol that you want to use.
- In the "Decimal places" box, select the number of decimal places that you want to display.
- Click "OK" to apply the changes.

Custom Date Formats in Excel

In Excel, you can format your date and time data in various ways using the built-in formats. However, sometimes, the default formats may not be suitable for your needs. In such cases, you can create custom date formats in Excel. Custom date formats allow you to display your date and time data in a format that is specific to your needs. For instance, you can display the date as "Monday, January 01, 2023" or "01-Jan-2023" or any other format of your choice.

Step-by-Step Guide:

- Open an Excel worksheet and select the cell or range of cells that you want to format.
- Right-click on the selected cell(s) and click on "Format Cells" or press "Ctrl+1" on your keyboard.
- In the Format Cells dialog box, click on the "Number" tab.
- From the "Category" list, select "Date" or "Time", depending on the type of data you want to format.
- From the "Type" list, select "Custom".
- In the "Type" field, enter the custom date or time format that you want to use. For example, if you want to display the date as "Monday, January 01, 2023", you can enter the following format: "dddd, mmmm dd, yyyy".
- (The characters used in the custom format are case sensitive. For example, "d" represents the day of the month while "D" represents the day of the year.)
- Click on "OK" to apply the custom format to the selected cell(s).
- You can also create custom date formats using a combination of built-in formats. For example, if

you want to display the date as "01-Jan-23", you can use the following custom format: "dd-mmm-yy". In this format, "dd" represents the day of the month, "mmm" represents the abbreviated month name, and "yy" represents the last two digits of the year.

Days in a Month

The "Days in a Month" trick in Excel allows you to quickly and easily determine the number of days in any given month, for any year. This can be very useful when you need to work with date calculations, project timelines, or other time-sensitive information in your spreadsheets. With this trick, you can avoid manually counting days or using external tools to determine the number of days in a month.

Step-by-Step Guide:

- Start by selecting a cell where you want to display the number of days in a month.
- Enter the year in another cell, for which you want to find the number of days in a month. For example, if you want to find the number of days in February 2022, you should enter "2022" in a nearby cell.
- In the cell where you want to display the number of days in the month, enter the following formula: =EOMONTH(DATE(year,month,1),0)-EOMONTH(DATE(year,month,-1),-1)
- Replace the "year" and "month" values in the formula with the cell references that contain the year and month values. For example, if you entered "2022" in cell A1 and "2" in cell B1, your formula should look like this: =EOMONTH(DATE(A1,B1,1),0)-EOMONTH(DATE(A1,B1,-1),-1)
- Press enter, and the cell will display the number of days in the month you specified.

Note:

- The "EOMONTH" function is used to find the last day of the month.
- The "DATE" function is used to create a date from the year and month values.
- The "-1" and "0" arguments in the "EOMONTH" function are used to find the last day of the previous month and the last day of the current month, respectively.
- This formula works for any month in any year, as long as the year value is entered correctly.

Default Chart

A default chart is a basic chart type that Excel creates when you select a data range and click on the "Insert Chart" button. It is a quick way to visualize your data and get a sense of the trends and patterns in it. Excel's default chart types include column, bar, line, pie, scatter, area, and more.

Step-by-Step Guide:

- Select the data range you want to visualize in the chart.
- Click on the "Insert" tab in the Excel ribbon.
- Click on the chart type you want to create in the "Charts" section (e.g. Column, Line, Pie, etc.).
- Excel will create a default chart based on the data you selected.
- Customize the chart as needed by selecting different chart styles, changing the chart layout, adding data labels or a chart title, etc.
- Modify the design of the chart by changing the colors, fonts, and effects to match your needs.

Tips for creating a Default Chart in Excel:

- To select multiple data ranges for your chart, hold down the Ctrl key while selecting the ranges.
- To change the chart type after it has been created, select the chart and then click on the "Change Chart Type" button in the Design tab of the Excel ribbon.
- To add or remove data from the chart, simply modify the data range you selected when creating the chart.
- To format the chart elements, such as the legend, axis titles, or data labels, select the element and

then use the formatting options in the Excel ribbon or right-click and select "Format."

Delete (Excel Shortcut)

The "Delete" function is a common task in Excel, whether it's removing a cell or a range of cells, a row, a column, or even an entire worksheet. Deleting a cell, row, or column can help to clean up your spreadsheet and remove unnecessary data that is not required. Using the "Delete" function can also be helpful when working with a large amount of data and trying to remove unwanted or incorrect entries quickly and easily.

Step-by-Step Guide:

- Open the Excel file that contains the data you want to delete.
- Select the cell, row, column, or range of cells that you want to delete.
- Press the "Delete" key on your keyboard or right-click on the selection and choose "Delete" from the context menu.
- In the "Delete" dialog box that appears, select the appropriate option:
    o "Shift cells left" or "Shift cells up": If you want to delete a range of cells and shift the remaining cells to fill the gap, choose this option.
    o "Entire row" or "Entire column": If you want to delete an entire row or column, choose this option.
    o "Worksheet": If you want to delete an entire worksheet, choose this option.
- Click the "OK" button to delete the selected data.

If you accidentally delete data that you did not intend to delete, you can use the "Undo" function (Ctrl+Z) to restore the deleted data.

Delete a Pivot Table in Excel

Pivot tables are a powerful tool in Excel for analyzing and summarizing large sets of data. However, if you no longer need a pivot table, it is important to know how to delete it properly. Deleting a pivot table in Excel will remove the pivot table structure and all associated data, but not the source data itself. This can help you clean up your Excel workbook and avoid clutter.

Step-by-Step Guide:

- Select the pivot table that you want to delete.
- Right-click on the pivot table, and select "Delete" from the menu.
- In the "Delete PivotTable" dialog box that appears, make sure that the "Entire PivotTable" option is selected.
- Click "OK" to delete the pivot table.

Alternatively, you can also use the following steps:

Select any cell within the pivot table that you want to delete.
- Go to the "PivotTable Analyze" tab on the ribbon.
- Click on the "Options" button in the "Actions" group.
- In the drop-down menu, select "Clear" and then "Clear All".
- Click "OK" to delete the pivot table.
- It is important to remember that deleting a pivot table will permanently remove all associated data and cannot be undone. Make sure to double-check before deleting a pivot table.

Delete Blank Rows in Excel

When working with large data sets in Excel, you may encounter blank rows that can cause confusion and make it difficult to analyze the data. Deleting these blank rows can help make your data easier to read and work with. The trick to delete blank rows in Excel can help you quickly and easily remove any blank rows in your spreadsheet, saving you time and effort.

Step-by-Step Guide:

- Open the Excel worksheet that you want to work with.
- Highlight the range of cells that you want to search for blank rows. You can do this by clicking and dragging your mouse over the cells, or by pressing Ctrl + A to select the entire worksheet.
- Click on the "Home" tab in the Excel ribbon.
- Locate and click on the "Find & Select" button, located in the "Editing" section of the ribbon.
- From the dropdown menu, select "Go To Special."
- In the "Go To Special" window, select "Blanks" and click "OK."
- This will highlight all of the blank cells in your selected range. Right-click on any of the selected cells and select "Delete" from the dropdown menu.
- In the "Delete" window, select "Entire row" and click "OK."
- This will delete all of the blank rows in your selected range.

Before deleting any data, it is always a good idea to save a backup copy of your original file in case you accidentally delete something you need.

Delete Cell (Excel Shortcut)

Deleting cells in Excel is a common task when working with data. The Delete Cell shortcut in Excel allows you to quickly delete the contents or formatting of a cell or range of cells without having to go through the usual right-click menu. This shortcut can save you time and make it easier to clean up your data.

Step-by-Step Guide:

- Select the cell or range of cells that you want to delete. You can do this by clicking and dragging your mouse over the cells, or by using your keyboard arrow keys to move the cursor to the cell or range of cells.
- Press the "Delete" key on your keyboard. This will delete the contents or formatting of the selected cell or range of cells.
- If you want to delete the entire cell (including any formulas, data, or formatting), you can use the "Delete" option from the right-click menu. Simply right-click on the cell or range of cells that you want to delete, and select "Delete" from the menu. You can then choose whether to shift the cells up or left to fill the gap left by the deleted cell(s).

When you use the Delete Cell shortcut in Excel, any data, formulas, or formatting in the selected cells will be permanently deleted. Make sure to double-check your work before deleting any cells, as this action cannot be undone.

Delete Hidden Rows in Excel

Sometimes, when working with large datasets in Excel, you may need to hide certain rows to make the data more manageable and easier to read. However, when it comes time to clean up your sheet, you may find that you need to delete these hidden rows. Unfortunately, you cannot simply select and delete hidden rows as you would with visible ones. Instead, you need to use a specific technique to delete hidden rows in Excel.

Step-by-Step Guide:

- Open the Excel worksheet that contains the hidden rows you want to delete.
- Highlight the rows above and below the hidden rows you want to delete. For example, if you want to delete rows 10-15, highlight rows 9 and 16.
- Right-click on one of the highlighted rows and select "Delete" from the drop-down menu.
- In the "Delete" dialog box, select "Entire row" and click "OK".
- Save your changes to the worksheet.

Delete Row(s) (Excel Shortcut)

Deleting rows in an Excel worksheet can be a time-consuming task, especially if you have a lot of data. However, using the delete row shortcut in Excel can significantly speed up the process. This trick will allow you to delete one or more rows with just a few clicks, saving you time and effort.

Step-by-Step Guide:

- Open your Excel worksheet and select the row(s) you want to delete.
- Press and hold the "Ctrl" key on your keyboard and then press the "-" (minus) key.
- A "Delete" dialog box will appear, select "Entire row" and click "OK".
- The selected row(s) will be deleted from your worksheet.

You can also use the delete key on your keyboard to delete a row(s), but it will not give you the option to choose between deleting the entire row or just the cell contents.

Delete Sheet (Excel Shortcut)

Deleting a sheet in Excel can be useful when you no longer need a sheet in your workbook or when you want to reorganize your data. It is a simple process that can be done using a shortcut key in Excel.

Step-by-Step Guide:

- Open the Excel workbook that contains the sheet you want to delete.
- Right-click on the sheet tab at the bottom of the screen that you want to delete.
- Click on the "Delete" option from the context menu that appears.
- A warning message will appear asking if you are sure you want to delete the sheet. Click "OK" to confirm.
- Alternatively, you can use the shortcut key "Ctrl + Shift + F" to bring up the delete sheet dialog box. Select the sheet(s) you want to delete and click "OK".
- The sheet will be deleted, and any data or formatting it contained will be permanently removed.

Be sure to save your workbook before deleting any sheets as the deletion is permanent.

Deselect Cells in Excel

In Excel, when you select cells, they are highlighted with a blue border to indicate that they are currently active. However, sometimes you may want to deselect cells to remove the blue border or to select a different range of cells. This is where the "Deselect Cells" trick comes in handy.

Step-by-Step Guide:

- Open an Excel worksheet and select a range of cells that you want to deselect.
- Press and hold the "Ctrl" key on your keyboard.
- While still holding the "Ctrl" key, click on any cell within the selected range to remove the blue border and deselect the cells.
- Release the "Ctrl" key to complete the process.

Alternatively, you can also use the "Esc" key on your keyboard to deselect cells.

- Open an Excel worksheet and select a range of cells that you want to deselect.
- Press the "Esc" key on your keyboard to remove the blue border and deselect the cells.

Note that these tricks only deselect cells within the current selection. If you want to clear the entire selection, click on any cell outside of the selection or press the "Ctrl" + "Shift" + "8" keys on your keyboard to remove the selection.

Display Units

In Excel, you can display numeric values in different units using the "Display Units" feature. This feature is useful when you want to show large or small numbers in a more readable format. For example, you can display a number in thousands, millions, billions, etc. instead of displaying the actual value. This makes it easier to interpret the numbers and makes your spreadsheet more visually appealing.

Step-by-Step Guide:

- Open the Excel spreadsheet that you want to work with.
- Select the cell or range of cells that you want to format.
- Right-click on the selected cell(s) and click on "Format Cells" or press the "Ctrl+1" shortcut key.
- In the Format Cells dialog box, select the "Number" tab.
- In the Category list, select "Custom".
- In the Type box, enter the code for the unit that you want to use. For example, if you want to display numbers in thousands, enter "0,K". If you want to display numbers in millions, enter "0.0,,". You can also add a currency symbol or other text before or after the code.
- Click "OK" to apply the formatting.

The number formatting code "0" represents a digit placeholder, "K" represents thousands, "M" represents millions, "B" represents billions, and so on. The comma symbol is used to separate the whole number and decimal places.

Does Not Equal Operator in Excel

The "Does Not Equal" operator in Excel is a comparison operator used to check if two values are not equal. It is denoted by "<>" and can be used in various scenarios where we need to check if two values are not the same.

Step-by-Step Guide:

- Open an Excel spreadsheet and select the cell where you want to use the "Does Not Equal" operator.
- Type in the first value you want to compare.
- Type "<>" (without the quotes) to denote the "Does Not Equal" operator.
- Type in the second value you want to compare.
- Press Enter to see the result. The result will be either TRUE (if the values are not equal) or FALSE (if the values are equal).

Alternatively, you can use the "Does Not Equal" operator as part of a formula. For example, you can use the following formula to count the number of cells in a range that are not equal to zero:

=COUNTIF(A1:A10,"<>0")

This formula will count all the cells in the range A1:A10 that are not equal to zero. You can replace "A1:A10" with the range of cells you want to count.

Draw a Line in Excel

Drawing a line in Excel can be helpful for highlighting trends, indicating targets or limits, or simply adding visual appeal to your worksheet. It's an easy way to make your data more understandable and accessible.

Step-by-Step Guide:

- Open your Excel worksheet.
- Click on the "Insert" tab on the top ribbon.
- Look for the "Shapes" icon in the "Illustrations" section and click on it.
- A drop-down menu with various shapes will appear. Select the line shape by clicking on it.
- Click and drag your cursor on the worksheet to draw the line where you want it to be.
- Release the mouse button when you have drawn the line to the desired length.
- To adjust the line's length or position, click on the line once. You will see several small circles on the line.
- Click on one of the small circles and drag it to adjust the line's length or position.
- To change the color or style of the line, click on the line and then click on the "Format" tab on the top ribbon.
- In the "Shape Styles" section, you will see various options for changing the line's color, thickness, and style. Choose the desired options by clicking on them.
- To delete the line, click on it and press the "Delete" key on your keyboard or right-click on the line and select "Delete" from the drop-down menu.

Remember, you can use this process to add multiple lines to your Excel worksheet. Just repeat steps 3-11 for each line you want to draw.

Edit Cell (Excel Shortcut)

Editing cells is a fundamental task in Excel. It enables users to change data that has already been entered in the worksheet. In Excel, there are several ways to edit cells, including the use of keyboard shortcuts. One such keyboard shortcut is the Edit Cell shortcut, which allows you to quickly edit the contents of a selected cell.

Step-by-Step Guide:

- Open an Excel worksheet and navigate to the cell you want to edit.
- Click on the cell to select it.
- Press the "F2" key on your keyboard. Alternatively, you can also press the "Ctrl" and "U" keys simultaneously.
- The cell you selected will now be in edit mode. You can make changes to the cell's contents, including deleting or adding text.
- After you have made your changes, press the "Enter" key on your keyboard to save the changes and exit edit mode.

If you want to cancel the changes you made, press the "Esc" key on your keyboard instead of the "Enter" key.

Excel Funnel Chart (Template + Steps to Create)

Editing cells is one of the most common tasks in Excel, and the Edit Cell shortcut can help you perform this task quickly and easily. This shortcut allows you to quickly edit the content of a cell without needing to double-click on it or use your mouse. This can save you time and make the editing process more efficient.

Step-by-Step Guide:

- Open Excel and navigate to the workbook that contains the cell you want to edit.
- Select the cell you want to edit.
- Press the "F2" key on your keyboard.
- The cell you selected should now be in edit mode, with the cursor positioned at the end of the cell's content. You can now make any changes or additions to the cell's content.
- Once you have finished editing the cell, you can press "Enter" to save your changes or "Esc" to discard them.
- Alternatively, you can use the arrow keys on your keyboard to navigate to a different cell while the current cell is in edit mode. This can be useful if you need to refer to other cells or data while editing.

Excel Funnel Chart (Template + Steps to Create)

A funnel chart is a type of chart in Excel that is often used to represent stages in a process and how they contribute to a final outcome. It is particularly useful when trying to visualize a process that has many stages, and when it is important to highlight the stages that have the greatest impact on the final outcome. In this tutorial, we will walk you through the steps to create an Excel funnel chart using a template.

Step-by-Step Guide:

- Open Excel and select a new worksheet.
- Go to the "Insert" tab and click on "Charts".
- In the "Charts" section, select "Funnel" chart type.
- A blank chart will appear on your worksheet. Now, click on the "Design" tab to open the Chart Tools menu.
- In the "Chart Styles" section, click on "More" to see more chart styles.
- Select a style that suits your data and click on it to apply it to your chart.
- Now, you will need to enter your data into the chart. Click on the chart to display the "Chart Data" window on the right side of the screen.
- In the "Chart Data" window, enter your data in the following format:
    - Stage 1
    - Stage 2
    - Stage 3
    - Stage 4
    - Stage 5
- Each stage will have a corresponding value that represents its impact on the final outcome.
- Once you have entered your data, close the "Chart Data" window.

- Now, you can customize your chart to suit your needs. You can change the colors of the chart, add labels, and change the font size and style.
- Once you are satisfied with your chart, you can save it by clicking on "File" and then "Save As".
- Name your chart and select the location where you want to save it.
- Click "Save" to save your chart.

Excel Gantt Chart Template

A Gantt chart is a type of bar chart used for project management that shows the start and finish dates of tasks on a timeline. The Excel Gantt chart template allows you to create a professional-looking Gantt chart that can help you visualize your project schedule and track progress.

Step-by-Step Guide:

- Open a new workbook in Excel.
- In the first row, create headers for the following columns: Task Name, Start Date, End Date, Duration, and % Complete.
- Enter the task names and start and end dates for each task in the appropriate columns.
- Calculate the duration of each task by subtracting the start date from the end date and enter it in the Duration column.
- Enter the percentage complete for each task in the % Complete column.
- Select the data range and insert a Stacked Bar Chart from the Insert tab.
- Right-click on the chart and select Select Data.
- In the Select Data Source dialog box, click on the Edit button in the Legend Entries (Series) section.
- In the Edit Series dialog box, select the Duration column as the Series Name and the Duration and Start Date columns as the Series values. Click OK to close the dialog box.
- Repeat step 8 and 9 for the % Complete column.
- Format the chart as desired using the Design and Format tabs.
- Save the template for future use.

To use the template for a specific project, simply enter the task names, start and end dates, duration, and % complete in the appropriate columns and the chart will automatically update to reflect the new data.

Fill Color (Excel Shortcut)

In Excel, you can fill the background color of a cell or a range of cells with a specific color. This can be useful for differentiating data or for adding a visual element to your spreadsheets. The Fill Color feature allows you to select from a variety of colors or create your own custom color to fill the selected cells.

Step-by-Step Guide:

- Open your Excel spreadsheet and select the cell or range of cells that you want to fill with color.
- Click on the Home tab in the Excel ribbon.
- Locate the Font group and click on the Fill Color button. This button has a paint bucket icon and is located in the middle of the group.
- A drop-down menu will appear with a selection of colors. Hover your mouse over each color to see a preview of how it will look on your selected cells.
- Click on the color you want to use to fill the selected cells.
- The selected cells will now be filled with the chosen color.

Customizing Fill Color:

- If you want to use a custom color, click on the More Colors option at the bottom of the color drop-down menu.
- The Colors dialog box will appear. You can select a color from the Standard or Custom tabs.
- To use a custom color, click on the Custom tab and use the color sliders or enter RGB values to create your desired color.
- Once you have selected your custom color, click OK to apply it to the selected cells.

Shortcut:

- Select the cell or range of cells that you want to fill with color.
- Press Alt + H + H on your keyboard.
- A drop-down menu will appear with a selection of colors. Hover your mouse over each color to see a preview of how it will look on your selected cells.
- Press the corresponding number key for the color you want to use. For example, 1 for a red fill color or 2 for a green fill color.
- The selected cells will now be filled with the chosen color.

Fill Handle in Excel

The Fill Handle is a useful tool in Excel that allows you to quickly fill a series of cells with data. It can be used for various purposes such as to copy formulas, fill dates, or create a sequence of numbers. The Fill Handle saves a lot of time and effort in data entry by automating the process.

Step-by-Step Guide:

- Enter a value in a cell.
- Select the cell(s) you want to fill.
- Position the cursor over the bottom right corner of the selected cell(s). The cursor will change to a black cross.
- Click and drag the cursor in the direction you want to fill the cells. Excel will automatically fill in the cells with a series of data based on the initial value.
- Release the mouse button to complete the fill.

The Fill Handle works with various data types, including numbers, text, and dates. However, it may not work with all data types, such as complex formulas or custom date formats.

Filter a Pivot Table in Excel

Pivot tables are a powerful tool in Excel that allows users to quickly summarize and analyze large data sets. One of the key features of pivot tables is the ability to filter data to focus on specific aspects of the data. Filtering a pivot table allows you to drill down into specific data subsets and analyze them in more detail.

Step-by-Step Guide:

- Open the Excel workbook that contains the pivot table you want to filter.
- Click on any cell within the pivot table to activate the PivotTable Tools contextual ribbon in the Excel ribbon menu.
- Click on the "Filter" dropdown button in the "Sort & Filter" group of the "Home" tab. This will display the filter dropdowns for each field in the pivot table.
- Click on the filter dropdown for the field you want to filter. This will display a list of all the unique items in that field.
- Select the checkbox next to the items you want to include in the filter. You can also use the search box to find specific items in the list.
- Click "OK" to apply the filter to the pivot table. Only the data that meets the filter criteria will be displayed in the pivot table.
- To remove the filter, click on the filter dropdown for the field you want to remove the filter from, and then click on "Clear Filter From [Field Name]". This will remove the filter and display all the data for that field again.

You can also use the "Report Filter" option to filter the entire pivot table by a specific field. To do this, drag the field you want to filter by to the "Report Filter" box in the "Fields" section of the PivotTable Fields pane.

Find and Replace in Excel

Find and Replace is a powerful feature in Excel that allows you to search for specific text or values within your worksheet and replace them with different text or values. This can save you a lot of time if you need to update a large amount of data in your worksheet. In this guide, we will go through the steps to use the Find and Replace feature in Excel.

Step-by-Step Guide:

- Open the worksheet where you want to perform the Find and Replace operation.
- Click on the "Home" tab in the Excel Ribbon.
- Click on the "Find & Select" button in the "Editing" section of the Ribbon.
- Select "Replace" from the drop-down menu.
- In the "Find what" box, type the text or value that you want to search for.
- In the "Replace with" box, type the text or value that you want to replace the found text or value with.
- You can also use the "Options" button to access more settings for the Find and Replace feature. For example, you can choose to match case or match entire cell contents.
- Click on the "Find Next" button to find the first occurrence of the text or value you are searching for.
- If you want to replace this occurrence, click on the "Replace" button. If you want to skip this occurrence and find the next one, click on the "Find Next" button again.
- You can also use the "Replace All" button to replace all occurrences of the text or value in one go.

Font Color with Custom Formatting

Excel provides numerous options to format the text, numbers, and cells in a worksheet. One of these formatting options is changing the font color. In addition to the standard font colors, Excel also provides the option to customize font colors using custom formatting. Custom formatting allows users to specify a font color based on the value of the cell. This can be useful in highlighting important data or in creating visually appealing spreadsheets.

Step-by-Step Guide:

- Select the cell or range of cells that you want to apply the custom font color formatting to.
- Right-click the selected cell(s) and click "Format Cells" in the context menu. Alternatively, you can press "Ctrl+1" to open the Format Cells dialog box.
- In the Format Cells dialog box, click on the "Number" tab.
- In the "Category" list, select "Custom."
- In the "Type" field, enter a custom format code. For example, to change the font color to red for any negative numbers, enter the code ";[Red]0;". The format code is made up of three parts separated by semicolons. The first part specifies the format for positive numbers, the second part specifies the format for negative numbers, and the third part specifies the format for zeros.
- Click "OK" to apply the custom font color formatting to the selected cell(s).

Custom font color formatting can also be applied to other types of data, such as dates or text. The format code for custom font color formatting will vary depending on the data type being formatted. It is recommended to refer to Excel's documentation or online resources for more information on custom formatting codes.

Format Painter

Excel's Format Painter is a powerful tool that allows users to copy formatting from one cell and apply it to another cell, saving a lot of time and effort when it comes to formatting data. With the Format Painter, you can easily copy formatting such as font style, size, and color, number format, cell borders, and more from one cell to another.

Step-by-Step Guide:

- Open the Excel spreadsheet and select the cell that has the formatting you want to copy.
- Click on the "Format Painter" button located in the "Clipboard" group on the "Home" tab. The cursor will change to a paintbrush icon.
- Click and drag the paintbrush cursor to highlight the cell or range of cells you want to apply the formatting to. Release the mouse button once you have highlighted the cells.
- The formatting from the original cell will now be applied to the selected cells.
- To turn off the Format Painter, press the "Esc" key or click on the "Format Painter" button again.

If you want to apply the same formatting to multiple cells or ranges, double-click on the Format Painter button instead of clicking it once. This will allow you to apply the formatting to multiple cells without having to click the Format Painter button again.

Formula Bar in Excel

The Formula Bar in Excel is a toolbar located above the worksheet that displays the contents of the active cell. It is useful for viewing and editing cell contents, especially when the content is too long to fit into the cell. This feature is available in all versions of Excel and can be a powerful tool for working with complex formulas and functions.

Step-by-Step Guide:

- Open a new or existing Excel workbook.
- Click on any cell to activate it.
- The contents of the cell will appear in the Formula Bar above the worksheet.
- To edit the cell contents, click on the Formula Bar and make changes as needed.
- To enter a formula or function, click on the Formula Bar and begin typing the formula or function. Excel will automatically suggest formulas and functions based on what you have typed.
- To exit the Formula Bar and save your changes, press the Enter key on your keyboard or click on any other cell in the worksheet.
- To cancel your changes and exit the Formula Bar, press the Esc key on your keyboard.

Formulas in Conditional Formatting

Conditional formatting is a powerful tool in Excel that allows you to highlight cells based on certain conditions. One of the conditions you can use to apply conditional formatting is a formula. This means that you can create custom formulas to apply conditional formatting to your data. Using formulas in conditional formatting can help you visualize your data and identify patterns or outliers.

Step-by-Step Guide:

- Select the range of cells you want to apply conditional formatting to.
- Click on the "Conditional Formatting" button in the "Home" tab of the ribbon.
- Select "New Rule" from the dropdown menu.
- In the "New Formatting Rule" dialog box, select "Use a formula to determine which cells to format" under "Select a Rule Type".
- In the "Format values where this formula is true" box, enter your formula. For example, if you want to highlight cells that contain values above 100, you can enter the formula "=A1>100", assuming that cell A1 is the first cell in the range you selected.
- Click on the "Format" button to choose how you want to format the highlighted cells.
- In the "Format Cells" dialog box, select the formatting options you want to apply, such as font color, background color, or border style.
- Click "OK" to close the "Format Cells" dialog box.
- Click "OK" again to close the "New Formatting Rule" dialog box.
- Now, the cells that meet the condition you specified in your formula will be highlighted

according to the formatting you chose. You can repeat these steps to apply additional rules with different formulas or formatting options.

Freeze Pane (Excel Shortcut)

Excel is a powerful tool for managing and analyzing data, but working with large datasets can sometimes be overwhelming. Fortunately, Excel has many features to help make working with large amounts of data easier. One of these features is the ability to freeze panes, which allows you to keep a certain row or column visible while scrolling through the rest of your worksheet. This can be especially helpful when working with large datasets that require a lot of scrolling.

Step-by-Step Guide:

- Open the Excel worksheet that you want to work with.
- Select the cell that is below the row or to the right of the column that you want to freeze. For example, if you want to freeze the top row, select the cell that is below the row that you want to freeze.
- Click on the "View" tab in the ribbon at the top of the Excel window.
- In the "Window" section of the ribbon, click on the "Freeze Panes" button.
- A dropdown menu will appear with three options: "Freeze Panes," "Freeze Top Row," and "Freeze First Column." Select the option that corresponds to the row or column that you want to freeze.
    - o If you select "Freeze Panes," Excel will freeze the selected cell and all cells above and to the left of it.
    - o If you select "Freeze Top Row," Excel will freeze the selected cell and all cells above it.

- o If you select "Freeze First Column," Excel will freeze the selected cell and all cells to the left of it.
- Once you have selected the option you want, Excel will freeze the specified row or column, and you can scroll through your worksheet while keeping that row or column in view.

To unfreeze panes, simply click on the "View" tab again, click on the "Freeze Panes" button, and select "Unfreeze Panes" from the dropdown menu. This will unfreeze any panes that are currently frozen in your worksheet.

Freeze panes only works when you are viewing your worksheet in Normal View or Page Break Preview. If you are viewing your worksheet in Page Layout View, the Freeze Panes option will be grayed out.

Full Screen (Excel Shortcut)

In Excel, full screen mode is a display setting that allows you to maximize the Excel window to fill the entire screen. This can be especially useful when you are working with a large amount of data and want to minimize any distractions on your desktop. The Full Screen mode in Excel is a shortcut that can help you to quickly switch between a normal view and a full-screen view.

Step-by-Step Guide:

- Open the Excel file that you want to view in full-screen mode.
- Click on the View tab on the Excel ribbon.
- Click on the Full Screen button in the Workbook Views group. Alternatively, you can use the keyboard shortcut, which is Ctrl + Shift + J.
- The Excel window will now be maximized to fill the entire screen.
- To exit Full Screen mode, click on the Exit Full Screen button in the top-right corner of the Excel window, or press the Esc key on your keyboard.

You can also use the Full Screen mode in Excel for presentations by creating a slideshow of your Excel data. Simply navigate to the View tab, click on the Full Screen button, and then use the arrow keys on your keyboard to move through your data.

Get Day Name from a Date in Excel

In Excel, dates are often used to record information about when certain events or transactions occur. However, sometimes it's useful to know the day of the week that a particular date falls on. For example, you might want to calculate how many Mondays or Fridays are there in a certain period of time. This is where the "Get Day Name from a Date" trick comes in handy.

Step-by-Step Guide:

- First, enter a date in any cell. For example, you can enter "2/28/2023" in cell A1.
- In the cell where you want to display the day name, type the following formula: =TEXT(A1,"dddd").
- Press Enter, and the day name will be displayed in the cell. In our example, the result will be "Tuesday".
- If you want to display the abbreviated day name, use the following formula: =TEXT(A1,"ddd"). This will give you "Tue" as the result.

Get Day Number of Year in Excel

In Excel, there are various functions that can be used to extract specific information from a date. One of such functions is the DAY function, which can be used to extract the day number of a date. However, to get the day number of a year, we need to use a combination of the DAY function and other functions like DATE and YEAR. In this trick, we will show you how to get the day number of a year in Excel.

Step-by-Step Guide:

- Open a new or existing Excel worksheet where you want to get the day number of the year.
- In the cell where you want to display the day number, enter the following formula:
- =DAY(A2-DATE(YEAR(A2),1,0))
- Replace A2 with the cell reference that contains the date for which you want to get the day number of the year.
- Press Enter to calculate the formula and display the day number of the year.
- The result will be a number between 1 and 365 (or 366 for a leap year), which represents the day number of the year for the date you entered.
- You can copy the formula to other cells by selecting the cell with the formula and dragging the fill handle to the cells where you want to copy the formula.
- The formula will automatically update the day number of the year based on the date in the cell reference you entered.

Get First Day of the Month in Excel (Beginning of the Month)

In Excel, you can use a formula to find the first day of the month for a given date. This can be useful when you need to analyze data on a monthly basis or when you want to create a report that starts on the first day of the month.

Step-by-Step Guide:

- Begin by selecting the cell where you want to display the first day of the month.
- Type the equal sign (=) to begin the formula.
- Type the EOMONTH function, which stands for "end of the month." This function returns the serial number of the last day of the month, which we will use to calculate the first day of the month.
- Within the EOMONTH function, enter the cell reference or date that you want to find the first day of the month for. This will be the first argument of the function.
- After the first argument, enter a comma (,) to separate it from the second argument.
- For the second argument, enter -1. This tells Excel to return the serial number for the last day of the previous month.
- Add 1 to the EOMONTH function. This will convert the serial number for the last day of the previous month to the serial number for the first day of the current month.
- Press Enter to complete the formula.

Get Quarter from a Date [Fiscal + Calendar] in Excel

In Excel, you can use a formula to get the quarter from a given date. This can be helpful when working with financial or sales data that is often broken down by quarter. There are two types of quarters that can be calculated: calendar year quarters and fiscal year quarters. Calendar year quarters are based on the traditional calendar year (January to December), while fiscal year quarters are based on a company's fiscal year, which may start and end at a different time.

Step-by-Step Guide:

- Open Microsoft Excel and create a new spreadsheet.
- In cell A1, enter a date in the format "mm/dd/yyyy". This will be the date you want to get the quarter for.
- In cell B1, enter the following formula to get the calendar year quarter:
=ROUNDUP(MONTH(A1)/3,0)

This formula divides the month by 3 and rounds up to the nearest whole number, which gives you the calendar year quarter.

- In cell C1, enter the following formula to get the fiscal year quarter:
=ROUNDUP((MONTH(A1)-MONTH(start_date)+1)/3,0)

Replace "start_date" with the start date of your company's fiscal year. This formula subtracts the starting month from the date's month, adds 1, and then divides by 3 and rounds up to the nearest whole number.

- Press Enter to see the result in each cell.
- If you want to copy the formula to other cells, use the Format Painter tool or drag the fill handle (the small square in the bottom right corner of the cell) to copy the formula to adjacent cells.
- To change the date, simply update the value in cell A1 and the quarter will update automatically.

Get Sheet Name in Excel

In Excel, a workbook may contain multiple sheets, and sometimes it's useful to know the name of the current sheet. For example, you might want to use the sheet name in a formula or in a cell reference. Excel provides a built-in function to get the name of the current sheet, which is called the "CELL" function.

Step-by-Step Guide:

- Open your Excel workbook and go to the sheet for which you want to get the name.
- Click on any cell to make it active.
- In the formula bar at the top of the Excel window, type the following formula: =CELL("filename")
- Press Enter to execute the formula.
- The cell will display the full path and name of the workbook, followed by the sheet name in brackets. For example: '[WorkbookName.xlsx]SheetName'
- To extract just the sheet name, you can use a combination of Excel functions: =RIGHT(CELL("filename"),LEN(CELL("filename"))-FIND("]",CELL("filename")))
- Press Enter to execute the formula.
- The cell will now display only the sheet name, without the square brackets or file name.

Get the File Name in Excel

In Excel, it's common to work with multiple files and it can be helpful to know the name of the file you're currently working on. Excel provides a function that allows you to get the file name and display it in a cell. This can save you time from having to switch between windows or checking the file properties.

Step-by-Step Guide:

- Select the cell where you want to display the file name.
- Type the following formula: =CELL("filename")
- Press Enter on your keyboard.

The formula will return the full path of the file along with the file name and sheet name, separated by brackets. For example: [C:\Documents\Excel Files[MyWorkbook.xlsx]Sheet1].

To only display the file name without the path and sheet name, you can use the following formula instead: =RIGHT(CELL("filename"),LEN(CELL("filename"))-FIND("]",CELL("filename")))

- Press Enter on your keyboard.

The formula will return the file name without the path and sheet name. For example: MyWorkbook.xlsx.

Get Years of Service in Excel

In Excel, you can calculate the years of service of an employee by subtracting the start date from the current date. This can be useful in various scenarios, such as calculating the length of service for an employee's record or determining the amount of service-based benefits they are entitled to.

Step-by-Step Guide:

- Open a new or existing Excel sheet.
- In cell A1, enter "Employee Name" to label the first column.
- In cell B1, enter "Start Date" to label the second column.
- In cell C1, enter "Years of Service" to label the third column.
- In cell A2, enter the name of the employee whose years of service you want to calculate.
- In cell B2, enter the start date of their employment in the format "MM/DD/YYYY". For example, if the employee started on January 1st, 2010, you would enter "01/01/2010" in cell B2.
- In cell C2, enter the formula "=DATEDIF(B2,TODAY(),"y")". This formula calculates the difference between the start date in cell B2 and the current date (i.e., today's date) in years. The "y" in the formula tells Excel to return the result in years.
- Press enter to calculate the years of service for the employee.
- To calculate the years of service for additional employees, repeat steps 5-8 for each employee, entering their name and start date in the respective cells.

The "DATEDIF" function is a hidden function in Excel. It stands for "date difference" and can be used to calculate the difference between two dates in days, months, or years.

Group (Excel Shortcut)

In Excel, the Group function is used to combine multiple rows or columns of data into a single summary row or column. Grouping can be useful for organizing large datasets and making them more manageable.

Step-by-Step Guide:

- Open your Excel worksheet containing the data you want to group.
- Select the rows or columns you want to group by clicking and dragging your mouse over them.
- Right-click on the selected rows or columns and click on "Group" in the context menu.
- In the Group dialog box that appears, choose the grouping options you want to use, such as the range of dates to group or the number of units to group by.
- Click "OK" to apply the grouping to your selected rows or columns.
- The grouped data will now appear in your worksheet with a collapsed view, showing only the summary information for each group.
- To expand a group and view its underlying data, click the "+" sign next to the group label.
- To remove the grouping and return to your original data layout, right-click on any grouped row or column and select "Ungroup" from the context menu.

Remember, using the Group function can be a powerful way to analyze data quickly and easily, but it's important to use it judiciously and not to over-group your data, as this can lead to oversimplification and the loss of important details.

Group Dates in a Pivot Table

In Excel, you can use pivot tables to analyze and summarize large amounts of data. One useful feature of pivot tables is the ability to group dates by month, quarter, year, or other custom time period. This can help you to quickly see trends and patterns in your data.

Step-by-Step Guide:

- Start by selecting the range of cells that contain your data.
- Go to the Insert tab and select PivotTable.
- In the Create PivotTable dialog box, select the range of cells that contain your data and choose where you want to place the pivot table.
- In the PivotTable Fields pane, drag the date field that you want to group into the Rows or Columns area.
- Right-click on one of the dates in the pivot table and select Group from the context menu.
- In the Grouping dialog box, choose the time period that you want to group by (e.g., Months, Quarters, Years) and click OK.
- Excel will automatically group the dates into the selected time period in the pivot table.
- To expand or collapse the grouped dates, click the plus or minus sign next to the date grouping in the pivot table.

If you want to group dates by a custom time period, such as every two weeks or every six months, select the By formula option in the Grouping dialog box and enter a custom formula.

You can also group date and time values by selecting the date and time fields separately and grouping them by the same time period.

Group Worksheets in the Excel

In Excel, grouping worksheets allows you to perform the same operation on multiple worksheets simultaneously. This can save a lot of time and effort when working with large workbooks that contain multiple worksheets. For example, you might want to print several worksheets at once or apply formatting changes to a group of worksheets. Grouping worksheets makes it possible to perform these tasks in one step rather than having to repeat them on each individual worksheet.

Step-by-Step Guide:

- Open the Excel workbook that contains the worksheets you want to group.
- Click on the first worksheet tab that you want to include in the group.
- Hold down the Ctrl key on your keyboard and click on the additional worksheet tabs you want to include in the group. You can click on as many worksheet tabs as you want to include in the group.
- Right-click on any of the selected worksheet tabs.
- From the context menu that appears, select "Group" option.
- You will now see that all of the selected worksheet tabs have been grouped together and have a white background.
- Any actions you take on one worksheet will be applied to all worksheets in the group. For example, if you apply formatting changes to one worksheet, the same formatting changes will be applied to all of the worksheets in the group.
- To ungroup the worksheets, simply right-click on any of the grouped worksheet tabs and select "Ungroup" option from the context menu.

You can only group worksheets that are next to each other. You cannot group worksheets that are not adjacent.

Grouping worksheets does not affect the data or formatting in the worksheets themselves, only the way they are displayed on the screen.

Hidden Cells

In Excel, it is possible to hide certain cells, rows or columns from view without actually deleting the data. This can be useful in a number of scenarios, such as when you want to temporarily hide some data from a client or boss, or when you want to focus on a specific part of your worksheet.

Step-by-Step Guide:

- Select the cells you want to hide.
- Right-click on the selected cells and click on "Format Cells".
- In the "Format Cells" dialog box, go to the "Protection" tab.
- Check the box next to "Hidden" and click on "OK".
- Now that the cells are hidden, you can protect the worksheet so that no one can unhide them without a password. To do this, go to the "Review" tab and click on "Protect Sheet".
- In the "Protect Sheet" dialog box, check the box next to "Hidden" and enter a password if you want. Then click on "OK".

Steps to unhide cells:

- Unprotect the worksheet by going to the "Review" tab and clicking on "Unprotect Sheet". Enter the password if you set one.
- Select the cells around the hidden cells. This will help you determine where the hidden cells are located.
- Right-click on one of the selected cells and click on "Format Cells".

- In the "Format Cells" dialog box, go to the "Protection" tab.
- Uncheck the box next to "Hidden" and click on "OK".
- The hidden cells should now be visible again. Protect the worksheet again if necessary by going to the "Review" tab and clicking on "Protect Sheet".

Hide and Unhide a Workbook in Excel

When working with multiple workbooks in Excel, it can become difficult to manage them all at once, especially when some workbooks contain sensitive or confidential information. In such cases, hiding the workbook can help prevent unauthorized access or accidental changes to the data. Additionally, hiding the workbook can also help declutter your workspace and improve your focus by removing unnecessary distractions.

Step-by-Step Guide:

- Open the workbook you want to hide.
- Click on the "View" tab in the ribbon at the top of the screen.
- In the "Window" group, click on the "Hide" button. Alternatively, you can use the keyboard shortcut "Ctrl + 1" to open the "Format Cells" dialog box, then click on the "Protection" tab and check the "Hidden" checkbox.
- The workbook will now be hidden, and its name will not appear in the list of open workbooks.
- If you want to unhide the workbook, click on the "View" tab in the ribbon again.
- In the "Window" group, click on the "Unhide" button. Alternatively, you can use the keyboard shortcut "Alt + F8" to open the "Macro" dialog box, then select the "Unhide" option and click "Run".
- Select the workbook you want to unhide from the list of hidden workbooks, and click "OK".
- The workbook will now be unhidden, and its name will appear in the list of open workbooks.

Hiding a workbook only makes it invisible from the list of open workbooks, but it does not protect it from being accessed by someone who knows its name or location. To secure your workbook further, you may want to consider using password protection or encryption.

Hide Axis Labels

Excel is a powerful tool for data visualization, and often we need to hide the axis labels to make our charts more presentable or to remove unnecessary clutter from the chart.

Step-by-Step Guide:

- Open the Excel workbook and select the chart that you want to modify.
- Right-click on the horizontal or vertical axis, and select the "Format Axis" option from the context menu.
- In the Format Axis pane that appears on the right-hand side of the screen, scroll down to the "Labels" section.
- In the "Labels" section, you will see options for "Label Position," "Label Contains," and "Label Options."
- To hide the axis labels, simply uncheck the "Labels" option under "Label Contains."
- Once you have unchecked the "Labels" option, the axis labels will disappear from your chart.
- Click on the "Close" button to exit the Format Axis pane and see your modified chart without the axis labels.

Hide Formula in Excel

When working with Excel, you may want to hide the formulas that you have used to calculate your data. This can be useful if you want to keep your data confidential or if you are presenting the data to someone who does not need to see the underlying calculations.

Step-by-Step Guide:

- Open the Excel workbook that contains the formulas that you want to hide.
- Select the cell or range of cells that contains the formula that you want to hide.
- Right-click on the selected cell(s) and select "Format Cells" from the context menu.
- In the Format Cells dialog box, click on the "Protection" tab.
- Check the box next to "Hidden" under the "Protection" tab.
- Click on the "OK" button to close the Format Cells dialog box.
- Now that you have marked the formula as hidden, you need to protect the sheet to prevent others from un-hiding it. To do this, go to the "Review" tab in the ribbon.
- Click on the "Protect Sheet" button in the "Changes" section of the ribbon.
- In the "Protect Sheet" dialog box, choose the options you want to apply. For example, you may want to allow users to select cells, but not make any changes to the worksheet.
- Set a password if necessary, then click on the "OK" button to apply the protection.

Hide Gap

When creating charts in Excel, you may encounter situations where there are gaps in your data. These gaps can make your chart look cluttered and difficult to read.

Step-by-Step Guide:

- Open the Excel workbook that contains the chart with gaps that you want to hide.
- Click on the chart to select it.
- Right-click on the chart and select "Select Data" from the context menu.
- In the "Select Data Source" dialog box, click on the "Hidden and Empty Cells" button at the bottom of the dialog box.
- In the "Hidden and Empty Cells" dialog box, select the option "Show data in hidden rows and columns."
- Click on the "OK" button to close the dialog box.
- Now that you have enabled the option to show data in hidden rows and columns, you can select the cells that contain the gaps that you want to hide.
- Right-click on the selected cells and select "Hide" from the context menu.
- Once you have hidden the cells with gaps, the chart will automatically adjust to hide the gaps as well.

Highlight Blank Cells

Working with data in Excel often requires identifying and highlighting specific cells or values. One common task is highlighting blank cells, which can help to identify missing or erroneous data.

Step-by-Step Guide:

- Open the Excel workbook that contains the data you want to check for blank cells.
- Select the range of cells where you want to highlight blank cells.
- Click on the "Home" tab in the ribbon.
- Click on the "Conditional Formatting" button in the "Styles" section of the ribbon.
- Select "New Rule" from the drop-down menu.
- In the "New Formatting Rule" dialog box, select "Use a formula to determine which cells to format."
- In the "Format values where this formula is true" field, enter the formula "=LEN(TRIM(A1))=0". Note that "A1" should be the top-left cell in your selected range.
- Click on the "Format" button to choose the formatting options for the blank cells. For example, you may want to choose a yellow fill color to highlight the blank cells.
- Click on the "OK" button to close the "Format Cells" dialog box.
- Click on the "OK" button to close the "New Formatting Rule" dialog box.

Highlight Dates Between Two Dates in Excel

If you have a large dataset in Excel that contains date values, you may need to highlight specific dates between two given dates. This can be useful for visualizing a specific range of dates or identifying certain trends or patterns in your data.

Step-by-Step Guide:

- Open the Excel workbook that contains the data with the date values you want to highlight.
- Select the range of cells that contain the date values.
- Click on the "Home" tab in the ribbon.
- Click on the "Conditional Formatting" button in the "Styles" section of the ribbon.
- Select "New Rule" from the drop-down menu.
- In the "New Formatting Rule" dialog box, select "Use a formula to determine which cells to format."
- In the "Format values where this formula is true" field, enter the following formula:

=AND(A1>=start_date,A1<=end_date)

replace "A1" with the top-left cell of your selected range and replace "start_date" and "end_date" with your desired start and end dates, respectively.

- Click on the "Format" button to choose the formatting options for the highlighted cells. For example, you may want to choose a blue fill color to highlight the cells.
- Click on the "OK" button to close the "Format Cells" dialog box.

- Click on the "OK" button to close the "New Formatting Rule" dialog box.

Hyperlink (Excel Shortcut)

Hyperlinks in Excel allow you to quickly navigate to a specific cell or range of cells within your workbook, to a different workbook or file, or even to a web page or email address. By using a keyboard shortcut to create hyperlinks, you can save time and work more efficiently.

Step-by-Step Guide:

- Open the Excel workbook where you want to create a hyperlink.
- Select the cell or range of cells that you want to hyperlink.
- Press the keyboard shortcut "Ctrl + K". This will open the "Insert Hyperlink" dialog box.
- In the "Link to" section of the dialog box, choose the type of hyperlink you want to create. For example, you can choose to link to a specific cell or range of cells in your workbook, to a different workbook or file, or to a web page or email address.
- Depending on the type of hyperlink you chose, enter the details of the hyperlink in the appropriate fields. For example, if you are linking to a web page, enter the URL in the "Address" field.
- If you want to change the display text of the hyperlink (i.e., the text that will be visible to users), enter the text in the "Text to display" field.
- Click on the "OK" button to create the hyperlink.

IF Cell is Blank (Empty) using IF + ISBLANK in Excel

In Excel, it is important to be able to identify whether a cell is empty or contains data. This can be useful for various reasons, such as calculating totals or averages without including empty cells.

Step-by-Step Guide:

To check if a cell is blank or empty using IF and ISBLANK in Excel:

- First, select the cell where you want to perform the check.

- Next, type the following formula into the formula bar:
=IF(ISBLANK(A1),"Blank","Not Blank")

In this formula, "A1" should be replaced with the cell you want to check. The formula will return the text "Blank" if the cell is empty or contains no data, and "Not Blank" if the cell contains data.

Alternatively, if you want to perform a specific action if the cell is blank or empty, you can use the IF function to create a conditional statement. For example, you can use the following formula to display the text "Empty Cell" if the cell is empty, and the cell contents if it contains data:
=IF(ISBLANK(A1),"Empty Cell",A1)

- In this formula, "A1" should be replaced with the cell you want to check.

IF Negative Then Zero (0) in Excel

The "IF Negative Then Zero" trick in Excel allows you to replace any negative value in a cell with zero. This can be particularly useful when working with financial data, where negative values may not be valid or desirable.

Step-by-Step Guide:

- Select the cell where you want to apply the formula.
- Type the following formula in the formula bar: =IF(cell_reference<0,0,cell_reference)
- Replace "cell_reference" with the reference of the cell containing the value you want to check for negativity.
- Press Enter to apply the formula.
- The formula will check if the value in the selected cell is negative. If it is, the formula will replace it with zero. If it is not negative, the original value will be retained.
- Copy and paste the formula to other cells in the same column, if necessary.
- The cells with negative values will now show zero instead of the original negative value.

This formula can also be modified to replace negative values with any other desired value by replacing the "0" in the formula with the desired value.

If the original value in the cell is not a number or is blank, the formula will return an error. In this case, you may want to modify the formula to include an additional check for these cases using the IFERROR function.

IFERROR with VLOOKUP in Excel to Replace #N/A in Excel

When working with large datasets in Excel, it is common to use the VLOOKUP function to find and retrieve data from a table. However, sometimes the VLOOKUP function returns an error message "#N/A" if it is unable to find the specified value in the table. This can be frustrating and can disrupt the flow of your work.

The good news is that Excel has a built-in function called IFERROR that can be used to replace the #N/A error with any value you specify, including zero or a custom message. This trick is especially useful when you have a large dataset and want to avoid manual error checking and cleaning.

Step-by-Step Guide:

- Open the Excel workbook and navigate to the sheet where you want to use the formula.
- Select the cell where you want to display the result of the formula.
- Type the following formula into the cell:
- =IFERROR(VLOOKUP(lookup_value,table_array,col_index_num,[range_lookup]),"replacement_value")
    - Replace "lookup_value" with the value you want to find in the table.
    - Replace "table_array" with the range of cells that contains the table data.
    - Replace "col_index_num" with the column number in the table from which to retrieve the data.
    - Replace "range_lookup" with either "TRUE" or "FALSE" to indicate whether

to find an exact or approximate match. If omitted, the default value is "TRUE".
    o Replace "replacement_value" with the value you want to display if the VLOOKUP function returns an error.
- Press enter to apply the formula to the cell. The result will either be the retrieved value from the table or the replacement value you specified in case of an error.

Increase and Decrease Indent in Excel

Indentation is a formatting tool used in Excel to modify the appearance of text. When you indent text, you can make it appear more organized and easier to read. Excel provides various options for indenting text, including increasing and decreasing the indent level of cells.

Step-by-Step Guide:

- Open your Excel workbook and select the cell or range of cells you want to indent.
- Right-click on the selected cell(s) and choose the "Format Cells" option from the context menu.
- In the Format Cells dialog box, select the "Alignment" tab.
- Under the "Indent" section, you will see two options: "Indent" and "Text control". The "Indent" option allows you to set the number of characters by which the text will be indented, and the "Text control" option allows you to choose the type of indentation you want to apply.
- To increase the indent level of the selected cells, click on the "Increase Indent" button located on the "Home" tab in the "Alignment" group. You can also use the keyboard shortcut "Ctrl+Shift+>" to increase the indent level.
- To decrease the indent level of the selected cells, click on the "Decrease Indent" button located on the "Home" tab in the "Alignment" group. You can also use the keyboard shortcut "Ctrl+Shift+<" to decrease the indent level.
- Click the "OK" button to apply the changes and close the Format Cells dialog box.

You can also use the indent buttons located on the "Home" tab in the "Alignment" group to indent cells without opening the Format Cells dialog box.

Insert a People Graph in Excel

Excel offers a variety of ways to present data visually, and one of those options is the People Graph. The People Graph is a unique graph type that allows you to display data in a more engaging way, using images of people to represent your data points. The People Graph is perfect for presenting data related to teams, departments, or any group of individuals you want to showcase in a visually appealing way.

Step-by-Step Guide:

- Open Excel and create a new workbook.
- Enter your data in a table format, including the categories you want to display in the graph and their corresponding values. For example, you might have a list of departments and the number of employees in each department.
- Click on the Insert tab on the ribbon at the top of the Excel window.
- In the Illustrations group, click on the drop-down arrow next to the Chart button, and select People Graph from the list of options.
- The People Graph dialog box will appear. In the left-hand pane, select the data range for your graph. You can also choose a layout style for your graph and select the image to use for your people.
- In the right-hand pane, you can customize the look of your graph by changing the colors, fonts, and other formatting options.
- Once you are satisfied with your settings, click the OK button to create your People Graph.

Your People Graph will now appear in your Excel workbook, and you can move it, resize it, and format it as needed. The graph will update automatically if you change the data in your table.

If you are not seeing the People Graph option in your version of Excel, it may not be available. The People Graph is currently only available in certain versions of Excel, such as Office 365 and Excel 2019 for Windows.

Insert an Arrow in a Cell in Excel

In Excel, you can insert different shapes to make your data more visually appealing and easier to understand. One of the shapes you can insert is an arrow. Arrows can be used to highlight a specific cell, draw attention to a particular data point, or indicate a trend.

Step-by-Step Guide:

- Open your Excel spreadsheet and navigate to the cell where you want to insert the arrow.
- Click on the "Insert" tab in the ribbon menu at the top of the Excel window.
- In the "Illustrations" group, click on "Shapes" and select the type of arrow you want to insert.
- Click and drag your mouse over the cell to create the arrow. You can also adjust the size and position of the arrow using the sizing handles and drag-and-drop functionality.
- To change the color or style of the arrow, right-click on it and select "Format Shape." In the "Format Shape" pane, you can modify the fill, outline, and effects of the arrow.
- Once you have finished editing the arrow, click outside of the arrow or press the "Esc" key to exit the drawing mode.

Insert Cell (Excel Shortcut)

In Excel, it's essential to add new cells in a worksheet, and there are several ways to do it. The traditional way is to right-click the cell where you want to insert a new cell and select the "Insert" option. However, there's a faster way to insert a cell using a simple Excel shortcut.

Step-by-Step Guide:

- First, select the cell(s) where you want to insert a new cell. You can select multiple cells by holding down the "Shift" key and clicking on the cells.
- Press and hold down the "Ctrl" key on your keyboard.
- While holding down the "Ctrl" key, press the "+" (plus) sign on your keyboard.
- A dialogue box will appear asking you whether you want to shift cells right, down, or entire rows or columns. Select your desired option and click "OK."
- The new cell(s) will be inserted, and the existing cells will shift accordingly.

Insert Current Date and Time

In Excel, it's often useful to record the date and time at which a particular event occurred, such as when a data entry was made or when a calculation was performed. Fortunately, Excel makes it easy to insert the current date and time into a cell using a simple shortcut.

Step-by-Step Guide:

- First, select the cell in which you want to insert the date and time.
- Next, press the "Ctrl" and ";" keys together to insert the current date in the selected cell.
- To insert the current time in the selected cell, press the "Ctrl" and ":" keys together.
- If you want to insert both the current date and time, you can combine the above shortcuts by first pressing "Ctrl" and ";" to insert the current date, then pressing the space bar, and finally pressing "Ctrl" and ":" to insert the current time.
- The date and time will appear as static values, meaning that they will not automatically update if the current date and time changes. If you want to have the date and time automatically update, you can use the "NOW" or "TODAY" functions instead.

Link a Single Slicer with Multiple Pivot Tables

Slicers are a powerful tool in Excel that allow you to filter data in a Pivot Table by selecting items from a list. However, if you have multiple Pivot Tables on a worksheet, you might need to use the same slicer to filter all of them. This is where the "Link a Single Slicer with Multiple Pivot Tables" trick comes in handy. This trick allows you to link a single slicer to multiple Pivot Tables, so that when you select an item in the slicer, all of the linked Pivot Tables will be filtered accordingly.

Step-by-Step Guide:

- Create a Pivot Table: Create the first Pivot Table on your worksheet by selecting the data you want to analyze, and then clicking "PivotTable" in the "Tables" group on the "Insert" tab.
- Add a Slicer: Add a slicer to the Pivot Table by clicking anywhere inside the Pivot Table and then clicking "Insert Slicer" in the "Sort & Filter" group on the "PivotTable Analyze" tab.
- Choose the Slicer Items: In the "Insert Slicers" dialog box, select the items you want to include in the slicer, and then click "OK".
- Duplicate the Pivot Table: Create the second Pivot Table on the worksheet by duplicating the first one. To do this, click on the Pivot Table, go to the "Analyze" tab in the ribbon, and then click "Options" in the "PivotTable" group. In the "PivotTable Options" dialog box, click "PivotTable" and then click "Create PivotTable". In the "Create PivotTable" dialog box, select "New Worksheet" and then click "OK".
- Link the Slicer to the Second Pivot Table: Click anywhere inside the second Pivot Table and then go to the "PivotTable Analyze" tab. In the "Filter

Connections" group, check the box next to the name of the slicer you created in step 2.
- Test the Link: Test the link by selecting an item in the slicer. Both Pivot Tables should be filtered accordingly.

Repeat steps 4-6 for any additional Pivot Tables you want to link to the slicer.

Lock Cells (Excel Shortcut)

In Excel, it is often necessary to prevent certain cells from being accidentally modified. This is where the "Lock Cells" feature comes in handy. This feature allows you to lock specific cells or a range of cells, preventing any further editing or modification.

Step-by-Step Guide:

- Open your Excel worksheet and select the cells that you want to lock.
- Right-click on the selected cells and click on "Format Cells" or navigate to the "Home" tab and click on the "Format" dropdown.
- In the Format Cells dialog box, select the "Protection" tab.
- Check the box next to "Locked" to lock the selected cells.
- Click on "OK" to close the Format Cells dialog box.
- Now, you need to protect the worksheet to ensure that the locked cells cannot be edited. To do this, click on the "Review" tab and select "Protect Sheet".
- In the "Protect Sheet" dialog box, you can set a password to unlock the worksheet or just click "OK" to keep it password-free.
- In the "Protect Sheet" dialog box, you can also select which elements of the worksheet should be protected. For example, you can allow users to select locked cells but not modify them, or you can prevent users from selecting locked cells altogether.
- Click on "OK" to finish protecting the worksheet.

Now, the selected cells are locked, and the worksheet is protected, preventing any accidental changes to the locked cells. To unlock the cells, simply unprotect the worksheet and uncheck the "Locked" box in the "Format Cells" dialog box.

Make a Copy of the Excel Workbook (File)

Making a copy of an Excel workbook (file) is important when you want to keep a backup of the original file or you want to create a duplicate file to work on without changing the original file. Excel provides an easy way to make a copy of a workbook.

Step-by-Step Guide:

- Open the Excel workbook that you want to make a copy of.
- Click on the "File" tab located in the top left corner of the screen.
- Click on "Save As" from the options on the left side of the screen.
- In the "Save As" dialog box, navigate to the location where you want to save the copy of the file.
- Enter a new name for the copied file in the "File Name" field.
- (Optional) Choose a different file format or file type from the "Save as type" drop-down list.
- Click the "Save" button to save the copy of the file.

Make a Paragraph in a Cell in Excel

Excel is a powerful tool that can be used for various purposes, including data analysis, creating reports, and making presentations. One of the lesser-known features of Excel is the ability to create paragraphs within a single cell. This can be useful for organizing information, providing detailed explanations, or making notes.

Step-by-Step Guide:

- Open an Excel worksheet and select the cell where you want to add a paragraph.
- Double-click on the cell or press F2 to activate the edit mode.
- Move your cursor to the position where you want to add the line break or paragraph.
- Press the shortcut key Alt+Enter. This will insert a line break within the cell.
- Repeat steps 3 and 4 to add more line breaks and create a paragraph.
- Once you have added all the necessary line breaks, press Enter to exit the edit mode and save the changes.

You can also use the formula bar to add paragraphs in a cell. Simply select the cell, click on the formula bar, move your cursor to the position where you want to add the line break or paragraph, and press Alt+Enter

Make Negative Numbers Red in Excel

Making negative numbers red in Excel is a helpful formatting trick that makes it easier to identify negative values in a spreadsheet. By default, Excel displays negative numbers in black with a leading negative sign (-) or in parentheses. However, by using conditional formatting, we can change the color of negative numbers to red, which can make it easier to read and understand a spreadsheet.

Step-by-Step Guide:

- Select the range of cells that you want to format (or the entire worksheet if you want to apply the formatting to the entire sheet).
- Click on the "Home" tab in the Excel ribbon.
- Click on the "Conditional Formatting" button in the "Styles" group.
- Select "New Rule" from the drop-down menu.
- In the "New Formatting Rule" dialog box, select "Format only cells that contain" from the "Select a Rule Type" section.
- From the "Format only cells with" drop-down menu, select "Cell Value."
- In the "Value" box, enter the formula "=A1<0" (where "A1" is the top-left cell in the selected range). This formula checks whether the value in the cell is less than zero (i.e., negative).
- Click on the "Format" button.
- In the "Format Cells" dialog box, select the "Font" tab.
- Under "Font Color," select "Red."
- Click "OK" to close the "Format Cells" dialog box.
- Click "OK" to close the "New Formatting Rule" dialog box.

- The negative numbers in the selected range should now be displayed in red.

If you want to change the color of positive numbers or zero values, you can repeat the above steps with a different formula in step 7. For example, to change the color of positive numbers to green, you can use the formula "=A1>0" and select green as the font color in the "Format Cells" dialog box.

MAX IF in Excel

In Excel, you can use the MAX IF formula to find the maximum value in a range that meets a specified condition. This formula is useful when you have a large data set and want to quickly find the highest value based on a certain criteria.

Step-by-Step Guide:

- Open a new or existing Excel worksheet.
- Enter your data set in a column or row. For example, let's say you have a list of products and their sales figures for each month of the year.
- Decide on the criteria you want to use to find the maximum value. For example, you might want to find the maximum sales figure for a particular product.
- Create a cell where you will display the result. This can be in the same worksheet or a different one. Let's say you want to display the maximum sales figure for a product in cell A1.
- In the formula bar, type the following formula: =MAX(IF(range=criteria, values))
- Replace "range" with the range of cells that you want to evaluate, "criteria" with the condition you want to apply to that range, and "values" with the range of cells that contains the values you want to return if the condition is met.
- For example, if your data set is in cells A2:B13 and you want to find the maximum sales figure for a specific product (e.g., "Product A"), you would use the following formula: =MAX(IF(A2:A13="Product A",B2:B13))
- Press Ctrl+Shift+Enter to complete the formula. This will create an array formula that calculates the maximum value based on the specified condition.

- The maximum value that meets the specified condition will be displayed in the cell where you entered the formula.

Merge – Unmerge Cells in Excel

Merging and unmerging cells in Excel is a useful formatting tool that allows you to combine multiple cells into one larger cell or split a merged cell back into individual cells. Merging cells can be useful when you want to center a title or heading across multiple columns or rows, or to create a table with merged cells. Unmerging cells can be useful when you want to separate previously merged cells into individual cells.

Steps to Merge Cells:

- Select the cells you want to merge. You can select cells that are adjacent or non-adjacent.
- Go to the "Home" tab on the Excel ribbon.
- Click on the "Merge & Center" button in the "Alignment" group. This will merge the selected cells and center the text within the merged cell.
- If you don't want to center the text, you can click on the "Merge Cells" option instead.

Steps to Unmerge Cells:

- Select the merged cell you want to unmerge.
- Go to the "Home" tab on the Excel ribbon.
- Click on the "Merge & Center" button in the "Alignment" group. If the cell is merged, the button will be highlighted in blue.
- Click on the drop-down arrow next to "Merge & Center" and select "Unmerge Cells". This will split the merged cell back into individual cells.

When you unmerge cells, any data or formatting that was in the merged cell will only remain in the top-left cell. If there was data or formatting in the other cells, it will be lost. So, be cautious when you are unmerging cells.

Merge [Combine] Multiple Excel FILES into ONE WORKBOOK

Combining multiple Excel files into one workbook is a useful trick that can save you time and effort when dealing with large amounts of data. Instead of having to open each file individually, you can simply merge them all into one workbook and work with them in a more organized manner.

Step-by-Step Guide:

- Open a new Excel workbook.
- Click on the "File" tab in the top left corner.
- Click on the "Open" option from the menu on the left.
- Browse for the first Excel file that you want to merge and click on it once to select it.
- Click on the "Open" button at the bottom right corner of the window.
- Once the file is open, click on the "Move or Copy" option under the "Home" tab in the ribbon.
- In the "Move or Copy" dialog box, select "New Book" from the "To book" dropdown menu.
- Click on the "OK" button to create a new workbook.
- Repeat steps 4-8 for each Excel file that you want to merge.
- Once you have created a new workbook for each file, click on the "Window" tab in the ribbon.
- Click on the "Arrange All" button in the middle of the ribbon.

- In the "Arrange Windows" dialog box, select "Vertical" or "Horizontal" from the dropdown menu under "Arrange".
- Check the box next to "Windows of active workbook" and click on the "OK" button.
- All of the open workbooks will now be arranged side by side in one window.
- Click on the "View" tab in the ribbon.
- Click on the "View Side by Side" option.
- Arrange the workbooks in the order that you want them to appear in the merged workbook.
- Click on the "View Side by Side" button again to turn off the feature.
- Click on the first worksheet in the first workbook.
- Click on the "Move or Copy" option under the "Home" tab in the ribbon.
- In the "Move or Copy" dialog box, select the new workbook that you want to merge the worksheet into.
- Check the box next to "Create a copy" and click on the "OK" button.
- Repeat steps 19-22 for each worksheet in each workbook that you want to merge.
- Once you have copied all of the worksheets into the new workbook, you can save the merged workbook under a new name by clicking on the "File" tab in the top left corner, selecting "Save As", and choosing a location and name for the file.

Merge Cells in Excel without Losing Data in Excel

Merging cells in Excel is a convenient way to combine multiple cells into a single cell. However, it can result in data loss if the merged cells contain data.

Step-by-Step Guide:

- Select the cells you want to merge. Make sure that the cells you want to merge contain data that you don't want to lose.
- Right-click on the selected cells and choose "Format Cells" from the context menu.
- In the "Format Cells" dialog box, click on the "Alignment" tab.
- Under the "Text control" section, check the "Merge cells" checkbox.
- Click "OK" to close the "Format Cells" dialog box.
- Now, the selected cells are merged, but the data is still intact.
- To view the data, click on the merged cell, and the data will be displayed in the formula bar.
- To unmerge the cells, select the merged cell, right-click, and choose "Format Cells" from the context menu.
- In the "Format Cells" dialog box, uncheck the "Merge cells" checkbox.
- Click "OK" to close the "Format Cells" dialog box, and the merged cell will be unmerged, and the data will be displayed in the original cells.

Merge-Unmerge Cells (Excel Shortcut)

Merging and unmerging cells is a useful feature in Excel that allows you to combine two or more cells into one cell or split a merged cell into its original cells. It can be used to create more organized and visually appealing spreadsheets.

Step-by-Step Guide:

- Open Excel and navigate to the worksheet where you want to merge or unmerge cells.
- Select the cells that you want to merge. You can select multiple cells by holding down the Ctrl key while clicking on the cells.
- Click on the "Merge & Center" button located in the "Alignment" group on the "Home" tab of the ribbon. This will merge the selected cells into one cell and center the contents.
- If you want to merge the cells without centering the contents, click on the drop-down arrow next to the "Merge & Center" button and select "Merge Cells" from the list.
- To unmerge cells, select the merged cell that you want to split into its original cells.
- Click on the "Merge & Center" button, and then click on the "Unmerge Cells" option in the drop-down list.
- The selected merged cell will be split into its original cells, and the content will be distributed across the original cells.

Excel Shortcut:

- To merge cells using a shortcut, select the cells that you want to merge.

- Press the "Alt" key on your keyboard and then press "H", "M", and "C" keys in sequence. This will merge and center the selected cells.
- To merge cells without centering the contents, press the "Alt" key on your keyboard and then press "H", "M", and "M" keys in sequence.
- To unmerge cells using a shortcut, select the merged cell that you want to split.
- Press the "Alt" key on your keyboard and then press "H", "M", and "U" keys in sequence. This will unmerge the selected cell into its original cells.

Military Time (Get and Subtract) in Excel

In some cases, you might need to work with military time, also known as 24-hour time format, in Excel. This is a timekeeping system in which the day is divided into 24 hours, starting from 00:00 (midnight) to 23:59 (11:59 PM). The military time format is commonly used in fields such as aviation, military, and healthcare.

Step-by-Step Guide:

- Open Microsoft Excel and create a new worksheet.
- In a cell, enter the time you want to convert to military time in the format "hh:mm AM/PM" (for example, "02:30 PM").
- Select an empty cell where you want to display the military time.
- Enter the following formula in the formula bar:
- =TEXT(A1,"hh:mm")
- Replace A1 with the cell containing the time you want to convert to military time.
- Press Enter. The military time value will be displayed in the selected cell.

Steps to subtract military time in Excel:

- In a cell, enter the first military time value in the format "hh:mm" (for example, "14:30").
- In a different cell, enter the second military time value in the same format.
- Select an empty cell where you want to display the time difference.
- Enter the following formula in the formula bar:
- =MOD(B1-A1,1)*24 & " hours"

- Replace B1 with the cell containing the second military time value, and A1 with the cell containing the first military time value.
- Press Enter. The time difference between the two military time values will be displayed in hours.

The MOD function is used to handle time values greater than 24 hours. The "&" operator is used to concatenate the result with the string " hours" to indicate the time difference in hours.

Month Name

In Excel, you can extract the name of the month from a date using a built-in formula. This can be useful when you want to display the month name instead of the date itself, or if you need to perform calculations based on the month.

Step-by-Step Guide:

- Enter the date in a cell where you want to extract the month name.
- Select the cell where you want to display the month name.
- In the formula bar, type "=TEXT(" followed by the cell reference of the date and ",") and then "mmm" (without the quotes).
- Press enter and the cell will display the month name in three-letter abbreviation format.
- If you want the full month name, use "mmmm" (without the quotes) instead of "mmm" in the formula.
- If you want to extract the month number instead of the month name, use "mm" (without the quotes) in the formula.

Make sure the date is in a proper format that Excel recognizes. If not, format the cell as a date. If you need to use the month name in a formula or calculation, make sure to reference the cell containing the formula, not the original date cell.

Month's Last Date

In Excel, we can use a formula to find the last date of any given month. This can be useful in financial reporting or any other data analysis that requires the use of monthly data.

Step-by-Step Guide:

- Open an Excel spreadsheet and select the cell where you want to display the last date of the month.
- Type the equal sign (=) to start a formula and type in the following formula:
- =DATE(YEAR(TODAY()),MONTH(TODAY())+1,1)-1
- Press enter, and the cell will display the last date of the current month.
- To display the last date of any other month, replace the TODAY() function in the formula with a date of your choosing. For example, to find the last date of December 2022, the formula would be:
- =DATE(2022,12+1,1)-1
- The cell will now display the last date of December 2022, which is December 31st, 2022.

This formula takes advantage of the fact that Excel stores dates as serial numbers, with January 1, 1900, being the first date. By adding one to the month and using the day value of one, we get the first day of the following month. Subtracting one day from that date gives us the last day of the original month.

Move a Pivot Table

Pivot tables are a powerful tool in Excel for analyzing data. When you create a pivot table, it appears on a new worksheet. However, you may need to move the pivot table to a different location in your workbook to better organize your data.

Step-by-Step Guide:

- Click on any cell within the pivot table to activate the PivotTable Tools contextual tab on the Excel ribbon.
- From the PivotTable Tools contextual tab, click on the "Move PivotTable" option in the "Actions" group. This will open the "Move PivotTable" dialog box.
- In the "Move PivotTable" dialog box, select the location where you want to move the pivot table to. You can choose to move the pivot table to a new worksheet or to an existing worksheet.
- If you choose to move the pivot table to a new worksheet, select the "New Worksheet" radio button and enter a name for the new worksheet in the "Location" field.
- If you choose to move the pivot table to an existing worksheet, select the "Existing Worksheet" radio button and then select the cell where you want the pivot table to be located. You can also specify a name for the worksheet in the "Location" field.
- Click the "OK" button to move the pivot table to the new location. The pivot table will be moved and any charts or pivot table reports based on the pivot table will be updated automatically to reflect the new location.

Move Data

In Excel, you may need to move data around your spreadsheet for various reasons such as organizing data, reformatting a table, or creating a new worksheet. The good news is that Excel provides a variety of methods to move data, and you can choose the one that suits your needs.

Step-by-Step Guide:

- Select the cells that you want to move. You can do this by clicking on the cell and dragging the cursor over the range of cells you want to move.
- Right-click on the selected cells, and then choose "Cut" from the context menu. Alternatively, you can use the keyboard shortcut "Ctrl+X".
- Click on the cell where you want to move the data to. If you want to move the data to another worksheet, click on the sheet name to switch to that sheet.
- Right-click on the destination cell, and then choose "Insert Cut Cells" from the context menu. Alternatively, you can use the keyboard shortcut "Ctrl+Shift+V". Excel will insert the cut cells and shift the existing cells down or to the right, depending on the direction you cut the cells.
- If you want to copy the data instead of moving it, use the "Copy" command instead of "Cut" in step 2. Then, use the "Insert Copied Cells" command in step 4.
- You can also move data by dragging and dropping. To do this, select the cells you want to move, click and hold the selection border, and drag it to the new location. When you release the mouse button, Excel will move the cells to the new location.

- If you need to move entire rows or columns, select the row or column by clicking on the row or column header, right-click on the selection, and choose "Cut". Then, right-click on the destination row or column header and choose "Insert Cut Cells" from the context menu.
- Finally, if you need to move data between workbooks, open both workbooks, select the cells you want to move, and follow the same steps as above to cut and paste the data to the new workbook.

Number of Months Between Two Dates in Excel

Calculating the number of months between two dates can be useful when working with financial data or when trying to determine the duration of a project or event. Excel has a built-in function that allows you to easily calculate the number of months between two dates.

Step-by-Step Guide:

- Open a new or existing Excel spreadsheet.
- In cell A1, enter the starting date of your time period. (e.g., "01/01/2022")
- In cell B1, enter the ending date of your time period. (e.g., "12/31/2022")
- In cell C1, enter the following formula: =DATEDIF(A1,B1,"m")
- Press Enter to calculate the number of months between the two dates.
- The result will appear in cell C1.

The DATEDIF function is not documented in the Excel help files, but it is a valid function in all versions of Excel.

Open Go To Option (Excel Shortcut)

The Go To function in Excel allows users to quickly navigate to specific cells or ranges within a worksheet. This function can save time and effort when working with large and complex worksheets.

Step-by-Step Guide:

- Open Microsoft Excel.
- Open the worksheet you want to work with.
- Click on any cell in the worksheet to select it.
- Press the F5 key on your keyboard. This will open the Go To dialog box.
- Alternatively, you can use the keyboard shortcut Ctrl + G to open the Go To dialog box.
- In the Go To dialog box, you can enter the cell reference or range you want to navigate to. For example, if you want to navigate to cell A1, simply type "A1" in the Reference field.
- Click on the OK button to navigate to the specified cell or range.
- You can also use the Special button in the Go To dialog box to navigate to specific types of cells, such as blank cells, cells with formulas, or cells with errors.

OR Logic in COUNTIF/COUNIFS in Excel

In Excel, we often need to count the number of cells that meet multiple criteria. One way to do this is by using the COUNTIFS function. However, sometimes we want to count cells that meet one criterion OR another. This is where the OR logic in COUNTIF/COUNTIFS comes in handy.

The OR logic in COUNTIF/COUNTIFS allows us to count the number of cells that meet at least one of several criteria. This means that if any of the criteria is met, the cell will be counted.

Step-by-Step Guide:

- Open Microsoft Excel and create a new or open an existing workbook.
- Select the cell where you want to display the result of your formula.
- In the formula bar, type "=COUNTIFS(" to begin the COUNTIFS function.
- Next, select the range of cells that you want to count.
- Type a comma "," to separate the first range from the first criteria.
- In quotation marks, type the first criterion that you want to count. For example, if you want to count cells that contain the word "apple", type "apple".
- Type a comma "," to separate the first criterion from the second criterion.
- In quotation marks, type the second criterion that you want to count. For example, if you want to count cells that contain the word "orange", type "orange".

- Type a closing parenthesis ")" to complete the COUNTIFS function.
- Press "Enter" to calculate the result of the formula.
- The cell will display the number of cells that meet at least one of the criteria.

You can add more criteria by repeating steps 7-9. Simply type a comma "," between each criterion.

Paste Values (Excel Shortcut)

When copying data from one cell to another in Excel, you have the option to copy the data itself or the data along with the formatting. However, sometimes you only want to copy the data without the formatting. This is where the "Paste Values" command comes in handy. It allows you to paste the values of a cell without any formatting, such as font size or color.

Step-by-Step Guide:

- First, select the cell or range of cells that contain the data you want to copy.
- Right-click on the selected cell(s) and choose "Copy" or press "Ctrl + C" on your keyboard to copy the data.
- Next, select the cell where you want to paste the values.
- Right-click on the selected cell and choose "Paste Values" from the menu or press "Alt + E + S + V" on your keyboard. Alternatively, you can also click on the drop-down arrow under the "Paste" button on the Home tab, and then select "Values" from the options.
- Excel will then paste only the values from the copied cells into the selected cell(s), without any formatting.

Percentage Format (Excel Shortcut)

In Excel, it's important to format numbers properly to ensure they are displayed correctly. The percentage format is commonly used when working with values that represent a portion of a whole. With this format, the number is multiplied by 100 and displayed with a percentage sign. For example, a value of 0.5 would be displayed as 50%.

Excel has a built-in shortcut to quickly apply the percentage format to a cell or range of cells.

Step-by-Step Guide:

- Select the cell or range of cells that you want to format as percentages.
- Press the "Ctrl" and "Shift" keys on your keyboard.
- While holding these keys, press the "%" key. This will apply the percentage format to the selected cells.
- Release all keys.

Alternatively, you can also use the following steps to apply the percentage format:

- Select the cell or range of cells that you want to format as percentages.
- Right-click on the selection and choose "Format Cells" from the context menu.
- In the "Format Cells" dialog box, select "Percentage" from the "Category" list.
- In the "Decimal places" box, specify the number of decimal places you want to display.
- Click "OK" to apply the percentage format.

Keep in mind that applying the percentage format to a cell does not change the underlying value. For example, if a cell contains the value 0.5 and is formatted as a percentage, it will display as 50%. However, the actual value in the cell is still 0.5.

Perform Two Way Lookup in Excel

Performing a two-way lookup in Excel allows you to search for a specific value in a table based on two different criteria, such as a product name and a date. It is a useful function in Excel that can save you time and effort when working with large data sets.

Step-by-Step Guide:

- First, select the cell where you want to display the result of the two-way lookup.
- Enter the following formula into the cell: =INDEX(range,MATCH(criteria1,range1,0),MATCH(criteria2,range2,0))
- Replace "range" with the range of cells that contains the data you want to search.
- Replace "criteria1" with the first criterion you want to use for the lookup.
- Replace "range1" with the range of cells that contains the data for the first criterion.
- Replace "criteria2" with the second criterion you want to use for the lookup.
- Replace "range2" with the range of cells that contains the data for the second criterion.
- The "0" in the MATCH function indicates that the function should perform an exact match.
- Press Enter to complete the formula.
- The result of the two-way lookup will be displayed in the selected cell.

Perform VLOOKUP in Power Query in Excel

VLOOKUP is a widely used function in Excel to search for a value in a table and return a corresponding value in the same row. However, when working with large data sets or complex data sources, VLOOKUP may not always be the most efficient solution. In such cases, Power Query can be a powerful tool to perform more advanced lookups, transformations, and data manipulations.

Step-by-Step Guide:

- Open Excel and load the data into Power Query: To load the data into Power Query, click on the "Data" tab in the ribbon and select "From Table/Range" or "From Other Sources" depending on your data source.
- Transform the data as needed: Once the data is loaded into Power Query, you can perform various transformations such as filtering, sorting, and removing duplicates. To perform VLOOKUP, you need to merge two tables based on a common column.
- Merge the tables: To merge two tables, click on the "Home" tab in the ribbon and select "Merge Queries" from the "Combine" group. In the Merge dialog box, select the first table, the common column to merge on, the second table, and the common column to merge on.
- Expand the columns: After merging the tables, you need to expand the columns that contain the values you want to retrieve. To do this, select the column you want to expand and click on the "Expand" icon in the "Transform" tab.
- Rename the columns: Once you have expanded the columns, you need to rename them to make

them more meaningful. To do this, right-click on the column header and select "Rename".

- Load the results: After you have performed all the transformations, click on the "Close & Load" button in the "Home" tab to load the results back into Excel.

Pictograph in Excel

Pictographs are an excellent way to represent data in a visually appealing and easy-to-understand format. They are commonly used to represent data related to population, sales, revenue, and other numerical values. Excel provides an easy way to create pictographs using conditional formatting.

Step-by-Step Guide:

- First, create a table with the data you want to represent using a pictograph. For example, if you want to create a pictograph to represent the sales data for different products, create a table with columns for product names and their respective sales numbers.
- Select the range of cells containing the data you want to represent with a pictograph.
- Click on the "Conditional Formatting" option under the "Home" tab.
- Select the "Icon Sets" option from the dropdown menu.
- Select the icon set that you want to use for the pictograph. Excel provides a range of icon sets to choose from, including shapes like circles, squares, and triangles.
- Choose the criteria for the icon set. You can choose to represent data with a 3-icon or 4-icon set, and set the minimum and maximum values for the icon set. For example, if you want to represent data using a 3-icon set, you can set the minimum value to 0 and the maximum value to the highest value in your data.
- Customize the icons used for the pictograph. You can change the color, shape, and size of the icons

to create a unique and visually appealing pictograph.
- Add a legend to the pictograph. A legend is a key that helps viewers understand what each icon represents. To add a legend, insert a text box or shape next to the pictograph and type in the relevant information.
- Finally, save and share your pictograph. You can save your pictograph as an image file, or copy and paste it into other applications like Microsoft Word or PowerPoint.

Pivot Table Formatting

A Pivot Table is a powerful tool in Excel that allows you to summarize and analyze large amounts of data in a simple and easy-to-read format. However, it's important to ensure that your Pivot Table looks clean and professional, which is where formatting comes in.

Step-by-Step Guide:

- Select the cell or range of cells that make up your Pivot Table.
- In the "Home" tab, click on "Format as Table" and select a table style that you like. This will give your Pivot Table a consistent look and feel.
- To add column or row headers, select the cell(s) you want to use as a header, right-click, and select "Format Cells". In the "Alignment" tab, check the box for "Wrap Text" to ensure your headers are fully visible.
- To change the font, size, and color of your Pivot Table, select the cell or range of cells you want to format, right-click, and select "Font". Here you can choose the font, size, and color that you like.
- To apply a background color to your Pivot Table, select the cell or range of cells you want to format, right-click, and select "Format Cells". In the "Fill" tab, choose the color you want to use as your background color.
- To remove subtotals from your Pivot Table, click on the "Design" tab in the Pivot Table Tools menu. Under "Layout", uncheck the box for "Subtotals".
- To hide or show grand totals in your Pivot Table, click on the "Design" tab in the Pivot Table Tools menu. Under "Grand Totals", select the option that you want.

- To apply conditional formatting to your Pivot Table, select the cell or range of cells you want to format, click on the "Home" tab, and select "Conditional Formatting". Here you can choose from a variety of options, such as highlighting cells that meet certain criteria or applying data bars to your Pivot Table.
- To add borders to your Pivot Table, select the cell or range of cells you want to format, right-click, and select "Format Cells". In the "Border" tab, select the border style, color, and width that you want to use.

Pivot Table Keyboard Shortcuts

Pivot tables are a powerful tool in Excel that allow you to summarize and analyze large amounts of data quickly and easily. While you can create pivot tables using the mouse and menus, using keyboard shortcuts can save you time and increase your productivity.

Step-by-Step Guide:

- To create a pivot table, first select the data that you want to summarize.
- Press the keyboard shortcut Alt + N + V to open the Create PivotTable dialog box.
- In the Create PivotTable dialog box, select the range of cells that contain your data and choose where you want to place your pivot table.
- Press Enter to create the pivot table.
- To move to the pivot table fields, press the keyboard shortcut Alt + J + T + F. This will select the first field in the pivot table.
- To move to the Values field, press the keyboard shortcut Alt + J + T + V. This will select the first value in the pivot table.
- To move to the Columns field, press the keyboard shortcut Alt + J + T + C. This will select the first column in the pivot table.
- To move to the Rows field, press the keyboard shortcut Alt + J + T + R. This will select the first row in the pivot table.
- To move to the Filters field, press the keyboard shortcut Alt + J + T + E. This will select the first filter in the pivot table.
- To expand or collapse a field in the pivot table, press the keyboard shortcut Alt + Shift + Right Arrow or Alt + Shift + Left Arrow, respectively.

- To move to the next or previous field in the pivot table, press the keyboard shortcut Tab or Shift + Tab, respectively.
- To refresh the pivot table data, press the keyboard shortcut Alt + F5.
- To clear the pivot table, press the keyboard shortcut Alt + A + C.
- To select the entire pivot table, press the keyboard shortcut Ctrl + A.
- To copy the pivot table, press the keyboard shortcut Ctrl + C.
- To paste the pivot table, press the keyboard shortcut Ctrl + V.

Pivot Table Timeline in Excel

Pivot Tables are a powerful feature in Excel that allows users to summarize and analyze large amounts of data quickly and easily. A Pivot Table Timeline is a tool that allows users to filter their Pivot Table data by date ranges in a visually appealing way. With this tool, users can easily track changes over time and make data-driven decisions.

Step-by-Step Guide:

- First, make sure your data is organized into a table with column headers. If it isn't, highlight your data and go to the "Insert" tab at the top of the screen and select "Table".
- Create a Pivot Table by selecting your data and going to the "Insert" tab at the top of the screen and selecting "Pivot Table". Choose where you want your Pivot Table to be located.
- In the Pivot Table Fields pane on the right side of the screen, drag the date column you want to use as your filter into the "Filters" box.
- Right-click on the date filter in your Pivot Table and select "Add Timeline".
- In the "Create Timeline" dialog box, choose the date column you want to use as your filter and click "OK".
- Your Pivot Table Timeline will appear. Click and drag the edges of the timeline to select the date range you want to filter your data by.
- Your Pivot Table will update automatically to show only the data within the selected date range.

Pivot Table using Multiple Files in Excel

Pivot tables are powerful tools in Excel that can help you analyze and summarize large amounts of data. However, it can be time-consuming to manually create a pivot table for each individual file.

Step-by-Step Guide:

- Open a new Excel workbook and click on the "Data" tab in the ribbon at the top of the screen.
- Select "From Other Sources" and then "From Microsoft Query".
- In the "Choose Data Source" window, select "Excel Files" and click on "OK".
- Browse to the folder that contains the files you want to include in the pivot table and select the first file.
- Select the worksheet you want to use and click on "Add".
- Click on "Close" in the "Add Tables" window.
- In the "Microsoft Query" window, drag and drop the fields you want to include in the pivot table to the "Criteria" pane.
- Click on the "SQL" button in the toolbar.
- In the "SQL Statement" window, enter the following SQL query:
- SELECT * FROM [Sheet1$]
- Replace "Sheet1" with the name of the worksheet you selected in step 5.
- Click on "OK" to close the "SQL Statement" window.
- Click on "File" and select "Return Data to Microsoft Excel".
- In the "Import Data" window, select "PivotTable Report" and click on "OK".

- In the "Create PivotTable" window, select the location where you want to place the pivot table and click on "OK".
- In the "PivotTable Field List" window, drag and drop the fields you want to use in the pivot table to the appropriate areas (rows, columns, values, filters).
- The pivot table will now update with the data from all of the selected files.

If you have more than one worksheet in your Excel files, you will need to modify the SQL query to specify the worksheet you want to use. You can also add additional criteria to the query to filter the data before creating the pivot table.

Print a Graph Paper in Excel (Square Grid Template)

Excel is a versatile tool that can be used for a wide range of tasks, including creating printable graph papers with a square grid template. With this feature, you can quickly create graph papers for sketching diagrams, drawing graphs, creating charts, and more.

Step-by-Step Guide:

- Open a new Excel workbook.
- Select the "Page Layout" tab from the ribbon at the top of the screen.
- Click on the "Size" button, and then select "More Paper Sizes" from the dropdown menu.
- In the "Page Setup" window that appears, set the "Width" and "Height" to your desired paper size. For example, if you want to create a standard letter-sized graph paper, set the width to 8.5 inches and the height to 11 inches.
- Under the "Print" section, set the "Margins" to "Narrow."
- In the "Page" tab, set the "Orientation" to "Portrait" or "Landscape" depending on your preference.
- Click on the "OK" button to save your changes and close the "Page Setup" window.
- Next, go back to the "Page Layout" tab and click on the "Gridlines" button.
- Select "More Gridlines" from the dropdown menu.
- In the "Format Gridlines" window, set the "Width" and "Height" to your desired grid size. For example, if you want to create a square grid

- with a 1/4 inch side length, set the width and height to 0.25 inches.
- Under the "Line Color" section, select "Solid Line" and choose a color for your grid lines.
- Under the "Transparency" section, set the transparency to 100% to make the grid lines appear faintly.
- Click on the "OK" button to save your changes and close the "Format Gridlines" window.
- You should now see a grid on your worksheet. If you want to adjust the size or position of the grid, you can do so by clicking on one of the corners of the grid and dragging it to your desired size and position.
- Once you are satisfied with your graph paper, you can print it by selecting "File" from the ribbon at the top of the screen, then "Print."
- In the "Print" window, make sure that the "Print Active Sheets" option is selected, and then click on the "Print" button.

Print Titles

Printing out a large Excel spreadsheet can be challenging, especially if it's a multi-page document. The column and row headings can quickly become lost in the mass of numbers and data. Print titles feature in Excel allows you to specify rows and columns that repeat on each printed page, making your spreadsheet more manageable and easier to read.

Step-by-Step Guide:

- Open the Excel file that you want to print.
- Click on the "Page Layout" tab in the Ribbon at the top of the screen.
- In the "Page Setup" section, click on the "Print Titles" button. This will open the "Page Setup" dialog box.
- In the "Sheet" tab of the "Page Setup" dialog box, you can specify which rows and columns to repeat on each printed page. For example, if you want to repeat the first row on every printed page, click on the "Rows to repeat at top" field and select the row(s) you want to repeat.
- Similarly, if you want to repeat the first column on every printed page, click on the "Columns to repeat at left" field and select the column(s) you want to repeat.
- Once you have selected the rows and columns you want to repeat, click on the "OK" button to save your changes and close the "Page Setup" dialog box.
- Now, when you print your Excel spreadsheet, the specified rows and columns will repeat on each printed page, making your document more readable.

Tips:

- You can use the same "Print Titles" feature to repeat both rows and columns on each printed page.
- You can also specify a range of rows or columns to repeat, by clicking on the corresponding field and selecting a range of cells instead of individual rows or columns.
- If you want to remove the print titles, go back to the "Page Setup" dialog box and clear the fields for the rows and/or columns to repeat.

Quickly Concatenate Two Dates in Excel

Concatenation is the process of combining two or more strings or values into a single string. In Excel, concatenation is often used to combine text strings or date values. Concatenating date values is a common task in Excel when you need to combine two dates into a single string.

Step-by-Step Guide:

- Open Microsoft Excel and create a new worksheet or open an existing one.
- Enter the two date values you want to concatenate in separate cells. For example, let's say you have a start date in cell A1 and an end date in cell B1.
- In a blank cell, enter the following formula: =CONCATENATE(A1," - ",B1)
- Press enter to see the concatenated result.
- If you want to use the "&" symbol instead of the CONCATENATE function, enter the following formula in a blank cell: =A1&" - "&B1
- Press enter to see the concatenated result.

R1C1 Reference Style in Excel

Excel offers two reference styles to refer to cells: A1 and R1C1 reference styles. While the A1 reference style is the default style, R1C1 reference style can be useful for advanced users who need to work with complex formulas and macros. The R1C1 reference style uses row and column numbers instead of cell addresses to refer to cells. In this trick, we will learn how to enable and use R1C1 reference style in Excel.

Step-by-Step Guide:

- Open the Excel workbook where you want to enable R1C1 reference style.
- Click on the File tab in the ribbon menu.
- Click on Options at the bottom of the menu.
- In the Excel Options dialog box, click on the Formulas tab on the left-hand side.
- Scroll down to the Working with formulas section and check the box next to R1C1 reference style.
- Click OK to save the changes and close the Excel Options dialog box.
- The R1C1 reference style is now enabled in Excel.
- To refer to a cell using R1C1 reference style, type "=R[row number]C[column number]" in the formula bar. For example, to refer to cell A1, type "=R1C1" in the formula bar.
- To refer to a range of cells using R1C1 reference style, type "=R[start row number]:R[end row number]C[start column number]:C[end column number]" in the formula bar. For example, to refer to the range A1:C3, type "=R1C1:R3C3" in the formula bar.
- You can use the R1C1 reference style in formulas, functions, and macros.

To switch back to the default A1 reference style, uncheck the box next to R1C1 reference style in the Excel Options dialog box.

Random Numbers

Excel provides a built-in function to generate random numbers. Random numbers can be useful for a variety of purposes, such as generating random data for testing or simulations, creating random samples, or selecting random winners in a contest.

Step-by-Step Guide:

- Open a new or existing Excel workbook.
- Select the cell where you want to generate a random number.
- Type the formula "=RAND()" in the formula bar and press Enter. This will generate a random number between 0 and 1.
- To generate a random number between a specific range, such as 1 and 10, use the formula "=RAND()*(10-1)+1". This formula multiplies the random number generated by RAND() by the range you want to use (in this case, 10-1), and then adds the minimum value of the range (in this case, 1) to shift the result up to the desired range.
- To generate multiple random numbers at once, drag the fill handle (a small square at the bottom right corner of the cell) across the cells where you want to generate random numbers. This will automatically copy the formula to the selected cells and generate a different random number in each cell.
- To recalculate the random numbers, press the F9 key or click the "Calculate Now" button in the "Calculation" group of the "Formulas" tab. This will generate new random numbers based on the RAND function.

1. **Randomize a List (Random Sort) in Excel**

Randomizing a list or performing a random sort in Excel is useful when you want to reorder a list of items in a random order. It is a useful feature in situations such as selecting a random sample from a larger dataset or creating randomized groups for an experiment.

Here's how you can perform a random sort in Excel.

Step-by-Step Guide:

- Open your Excel worksheet and select the range of cells that you want to randomize.
- Click on the "Data" tab in the ribbon at the top of the Excel window.
- Click on the "Sort" button in the "Sort & Filter" section of the ribbon. This will open the "Sort" dialog box.
- In the "Sort" dialog box, click on the drop-down arrow next to the "Sort by" field and select "Custom List".
- In the "Custom Lists" dialog box, click on "NEW LIST".
- Type in the values in the order you want them to be randomized, separated by commas. For example, if you want to randomize a list of names, you could type "John, Jane, Mark, Sarah".
- Click "Add" to add your list to the Custom Lists box, then click "OK" to close the Custom Lists dialog box.
- Back in the Sort dialog box, click on the "Order" drop-down and select "Custom List".
- In the "Custom Lists" drop-down, select the list you just created, then click "OK".
- Finally, click "OK" again in the Sort dialog box to apply the random sort to your selected range of cells.

Recover Unsaved Excel Files When Excel Crashed

Excel is a widely used application for managing data and creating spreadsheets. Sometimes, due to unforeseen circumstances, Excel might crash, leading to the loss of unsaved work. In such situations, it can be helpful to know how to recover unsaved Excel files.

Step-by-Step Guide:

- Open Excel and click on the "File" tab in the top left corner of the screen.
- Click on "Open" in the left-hand menu.
- Click on the "Recent Workbooks" option at the bottom of the window.
- Scroll down to the "Recover Unsaved Workbooks" option and click on it.
- Select the unsaved workbook you want to recover from the list of available files.
- Click on "Open" to open the recovered file.
- Save the recovered file to your computer to ensure you do not lose any changes made to the document.

If the above steps do not work, you can also try searching for the unsaved file using Windows File Explorer. Go to "Documents" > "My Documents" > "Unsaved Files" to see if the file is available.

Refresh a Pivot Table

A Pivot Table is a powerful tool in Excel that allows you to summarize and analyze large amounts of data quickly and easily. However, the data in a Pivot Table is not updated automatically, which means that if the data source changes, the Pivot Table may not show the latest information. To update or refresh a Pivot Table, you need to use the Refresh command.

Step-by-Step Guide:

- Open the Excel workbook that contains the Pivot Table you want to refresh.
- Click on the Pivot Table you want to refresh to select it.
- In the PivotTable Analyze or Options tab (depending on the version of Excel you are using), click on the "Refresh" button.
- If you have Excel 365 or later versions, you can also right-click on the Pivot Table and select "Refresh" from the drop-down menu.
- Wait for Excel to update the Pivot Table with the latest data from the data source.
- Check if the Pivot Table is updated with the latest data.
- If the Pivot Table is still not updated, try refreshing the data source or checking if the data source has any issues.

Refresh All Pivot Tables at Once in Excel

Pivot tables are a powerful tool in Excel that allow you to summarize and analyze large amounts of data. When you have multiple pivot tables in your workbook, you may need to refresh them all at once after making changes to the source data. Manually refreshing each pivot table can be time-consuming and tedious, but Excel provides a quick and easy way to refresh all pivot tables at once using a keyboard shortcut.

Step-by-Step Guide:

- Open your Excel workbook that contains multiple pivot tables that you want to refresh.
- Make sure that you are on the worksheet that contains the pivot tables.
- Press the "Alt + F5" keys on your keyboard. This will open the "Refresh All" dialog box.
- In the "Refresh All" dialog box, make sure that "Refresh all connections" option is selected.
- Click the "OK" button. Excel will refresh all pivot tables in the workbook.

You can also refresh all pivot tables by clicking the "Refresh All" button on the "Data" tab of the Excel ribbon.

Remove Drop Down List (Data validation) in Excel

Excel provides a feature called data validation that helps users create drop-down lists for cells. These lists can make data entry more efficient and consistent by allowing users to select values from a predefined set. However, there may be situations where you need to remove the drop-down list from a cell or a range of cells. This could be because you no longer need the list, or you want to replace it with a different list. In such cases, you can use the steps outlined below to remove the drop-down list from your cells.

Step-by-Step Guide:

- Open the Excel file that contains the drop-down list you want to remove.
- Select the cell or range of cells containing the drop-down list.
- Click on the "Data" tab in the ribbon menu.
- Click on "Data Validation" in the "Data Tools" group.
- In the "Data Validation" dialog box that appears, select the "Settings" tab.
- In the "Allow" drop-down menu, select "Any value".
- Click on the "OK" button to close the dialog box.
- The drop-down list will now be removed from the selected cell or range of cells.

If you have multiple cells with drop-down lists, you can select them all at once before following the steps above.

Remove Pagebreak in Excel

In Microsoft Excel, page breaks are used to specify where a new page will begin when the document is printed. By default, Excel automatically inserts page breaks based on the page size and margin settings. However, sometimes these page breaks may not be in the desired location, causing unwanted blank spaces or cutting off important data. In this case, you may want to remove a page break.

Step-by-Step Guide:

- Open the worksheet where you want to remove the page break.
- Go to the "View" tab on the ribbon at the top of the Excel window.
- In the "Workbook Views" section, click on the "Page Break Preview" button. This will change the view to show where the page breaks are located.
- Click on the page break line that you want to remove. The page break line will be highlighted with a thick blue border when selected.
- Press the "Delete" key on your keyboard to remove the selected page break.
- Repeat steps 4 and 5 for any additional page breaks you want to remove.
- Once you've finished removing page breaks, click on the "Normal" button in the "Workbook Views" section of the ribbon to switch back to the normal worksheet view.

Reverse VLOOKUP

VLOOKUP is a popular function in Excel that allows you to search for a value in the first column of a table and return a value in the same row from another column. However, sometimes you may need to do the opposite, i.e., search for a value in a column and return a value from the first column. In this case, you can use the reverse VLOOKUP function, also known as INDEX-MATCH function.

Step-by-Step Guide:

- Open the Excel file and select a blank cell where you want to display the result of the Reverse VLOOKUP function.
- Type the following formula in the selected cell: =INDEX(Table_array,MATCH(lookup_value,lookup_array,0),1) Replace "Table_array" with the range of cells that contains the data you want to search, "lookup_value" with the value you want to find, and "lookup_array" with the range of cells that contains the column you want to search.
- Press the Enter key to apply the formula.
- The result of the Reverse VLOOKUP function will be displayed in the selected cell.

Root of Number

In Excel, you can easily find the root of a number using a simple formula. The root of a number refers to the value that when multiplied by itself a certain number of times gives the original number. For example, the square root of 16 is 4, since 4 x 4 = 16.

Step-by-Step Guide:

- Enter the number you want to find the root of in a cell.
- Decide which root you want to find. If you want to find the square root, use the formula =SQRT(cell number) where cell number is the reference to the cell containing the original number. For example, if the original number is in cell A1, you would use the formula =SQRT(A1).
- If you want to find the cube root or any other root, use the formula =cell number^(1/n) where cell number is the reference to the cell containing the original number and n is the root you want to find. For example, if the original number is in cell A1 and you want to find the cube root, you would use the formula =A1^(1/3).
- Press Enter to calculate the root value.
- The result will be displayed in the cell where you entered the formula.

Rotate Text in Excel (Text Orientation)

Rotating text in Excel is a useful formatting technique that can be used to make your data more readable and visually appealing. It allows you to change the orientation of the text in a cell to make it appear vertically or at an angle. This can be especially useful when you have limited space in your worksheet, and you want to fit more text into a cell without making the cell wider.

Step-by-Step Guide:

- Open your Excel worksheet and select the cell(s) that you want to rotate the text for.
- Click on the "Home" tab in the Excel ribbon menu.
- Look for the "Alignment" section in the ribbon and click on the "Orientation" button. It is represented by a slanted letter A.
- A drop-down menu will appear. You can choose any of the predefined text orientations from the menu, or you can click on "More Orientation Options" at the bottom of the list to see more choices.
- In the "Format Cells" dialog box that appears, click on the "Alignment" tab.
- Under the "Text control" section, you will see the "Orientation" group. Here you can adjust the degree of rotation by typing a value into the "Degrees" box, or you can use the arrow buttons to rotate the text clockwise or counterclockwise.
- Once you have selected the desired orientation, click "OK" to close the dialog box and apply the changes to your selected cell(s).
- Your text should now appear rotated in the cell(s) you selected.

Round a Number to Nearest 1000, 100, and 10 in Excel

Excel provides various functions to round off numbers to the nearest multiple of 10, 100, 1000, and so on. This trick can come in handy when you need to simplify data visualization or presentation. For instance, if you have a long list of numbers and want to display them in a simpler format, rounding them to the nearest 100 or 1000 can help.

Step-by-Step Guide:

- Open Microsoft Excel and create a new workbook or open an existing one where you want to round off numbers.
- Enter the numbers that you want to round off in a new column or select the existing column.
- Select the cell where you want to display the rounded number.
- Type "=ROUND(number, -3)" to round off the number to the nearest 1000. Replace "number" with the cell address of the number you want to round off.
- Press "Enter" to apply the formula.
- To round off the number to the nearest 100, type "=ROUND(number, -2)". Replace "number" with the cell address of the number you want to round off.
- Press "Enter" to apply the formula.
- To round off the number to the nearest 10, type "=ROUND(number, -1)". Replace "number" with the cell address of the number you want to round off.
- Press "Enter" to apply the formula.

The second argument in the ROUND function represents the number of digits to which you want to round the number. A negative value of the second argument rounds off the number to the left of the decimal point.

Round to Nearest .5, 5. 50 (Down-Up) in Excel

In Excel, you can round numbers to the nearest .5, 5 or 50 using the ROUND function. This trick can come in handy when you are dealing with numbers that require more specific rounding. The ROUND function rounds a number to a specified number of digits. By using the ROUND function with specific values, you can round your numbers to the nearest .5, 5 or 50.

Step-by-Step Guide:

- Open a new or existing Excel spreadsheet where you want to apply the rounding formula.
- Select the cell(s) that contain the numbers you want to round.
- In the formula bar, type "=ROUND(" and then select the cell(s) containing the number(s) you want to round.
- After the cell reference, type a comma "," to separate the arguments of the function.
- Type the number of decimal places you want to round to, followed by a comma.
- After the comma, enter either ".5", "5", or "50" depending on the desired rounding factor, followed by a ")" to close the function.
- Press "Enter" to apply the formula and round the number(s) to the desired value.

Row Vs Column in Excel (Difference)

In Excel, rows and columns are two fundamental components that help organize and structure data. They are used to categorize and store information in a systematic and easy-to-read manner. Rows run horizontally, whereas columns run vertically.

Step-by-Step Guide:

- Open an Excel worksheet.
- Navigate to the top-left corner of the worksheet where row headings and column headings intersect.
- Identify the first row, which is labeled as "1". This row runs horizontally across the worksheet.
- Identify the first column, which is labeled as "A". This column runs vertically down the worksheet.
- Notice that each row is identified by a number, and each column is identified by a letter.
- The intersection of a row and a column is called a cell.
- Rows are typically used to group or categorize data horizontally, such as by date or product.
- Columns are typically used to group or categorize data vertically, such as by category or description.
- It is important to understand the difference between rows and columns to effectively organize and analyze data in Excel.
- Experiment with entering data into different rows and columns to get a better understanding of how they work.

Save Excel File (Workbook) as CSV (XLSX TO CSV)

Saving an Excel file as a CSV (Comma Separated Values) file allows you to share your data with others who may not have access to Excel. A CSV file can be opened in any text editor or spreadsheet program, making it a universal format for data exchange.

Step-by-Step Guide:

- Open the Excel file (workbook) that you want to save as a CSV file.
- Click on the "File" tab in the top left corner of the screen.
- Click on "Save As" from the options on the left-hand side.
- In the "Save As" dialog box, navigate to the folder where you want to save the CSV file.
- In the "Save as type" dropdown menu, select "CSV (Comma delimited) (*.csv)".
- Type a name for your CSV file in the "File name" field.
- Click the "Save" button.

Select Non-Continues Cells

In Excel, we often need to select cells that are not in a continuous range. This can be a bit tricky since we can't use the usual click and drag method to select cells that are not adjacent. However, there are several ways to select non-continuous cells in Excel, which we will discuss in this guide.

Step-by-Step Guide:

- First, open the Excel workbook that contains the cells you want to select.
- Click on the first cell that you want to select.
- Press and hold the "Ctrl" key on your keyboard.
- While holding the "Ctrl" key, click on each additional cell that you want to select. You can select cells that are not adjacent to each other by clicking on them individually while holding down the "Ctrl" key.
- Once you have selected all the cells you want to work with, release the "Ctrl" key.
- You can now perform any desired operation on the selected cells, such as formatting, editing, or copying and pasting to another location.
- If you need to add additional cells to your selection, simply hold down the "Ctrl" key and click on each additional cell you want to add.
- If you accidentally select a cell that you don't want to include in your selection, simply hold down the "Ctrl" key and click on the cell to deselect it.
- Once you have finished working with your selected cells, you can deselect them by clicking anywhere outside of the selected area or by pressing the "Esc" key on your keyboard.

Another way to select non-continuous cells is to use the "Name Box" feature in Excel. Simply type the cell references you want to select, separated by commas, into the Name Box and press Enter. This will select all the specified cells at once.

Select Row (Excel Shortcut)

Navigating through large spreadsheets can be time-consuming, especially when trying to select specific rows. Using a keyboard shortcut to select a row in Excel can save you time and make working with spreadsheets more efficient.

Step-by-Step Guide:

- Open your Excel spreadsheet.
- Navigate to the worksheet that contains the row you want to select.
- Move the cursor to the left of the row you want to select. The cursor should turn into a right-facing arrow.
- Press the Shift key and the Spacebar at the same time to select the entire row.
- The selected row will now be highlighted in blue.

If you want to select multiple rows at once, you can hold down the Shift key and use the arrow keys to navigate to the other rows you want to select before releasing the Shift key and Spacebar.

Sentence Case

When you have a block of text in Microsoft Excel that is in all caps or lowercase, and you want to convert it into sentence case where only the first letter of each sentence is capitalized, you can use the "Sentence Case" function. This will help make your text more readable and presentable.

Step-by-Step Guide:

- Open the Excel worksheet that contains the text you want to change to sentence case.
- Select the cell or range of cells that contain the text you want to change.
- In the formula bar at the top of the screen, type the following formula: =PROPER(A1)
- Press Enter on your keyboard.
- The text in the selected cells will now be converted to sentence case.

If the text you want to convert to sentence case is in a different cell than A1, you will need to adjust the formula accordingly. For example, if the text is in cell B2, the formula should be =PROPER(B2).

Separate Date and Time in Excel

Separating date and time is a common task in Excel when you have date and time combined in a single cell. You might need to separate them to perform further calculations or analysis. Fortunately, Excel provides an easy way to separate date and time using text functions.

Step-by-Step Guide:

- Open the Excel file containing the date and time values that you want to separate.
- Select the cell or range of cells containing the date and time values.
- Right-click on the selected cell(s) and click on "Format Cells".
- In the Format Cells dialog box, select the "Custom" category.
- In the "Type" field, enter the desired format for your date and time values, such as "mm/dd/yyyy hh:mm AM/PM". Click OK to save the format changes.
- In a new column next to the column containing the combined date and time values, type the following formula: =LEFT(A2,FIND(" ",A2)-1). Replace "A2" with the cell reference of the combined date and time value you want to separate.
- Press Enter to apply the formula to the first cell in the new column.
- Drag the fill handle of the cell containing the formula down to the last row of your data to apply the formula to all cells in the column.
- Now, in the next column, type the following formula: =RIGHT(A2,LEN(A2)-FIND(" ",A2)). Replace "A2" with the cell reference of the

combined date and time value you want to separate.
- Press Enter to apply the formula to the first cell in the new column.
- Drag the fill handle of the cell containing the formula down to the last row of your data to apply the formula to all cells in the column.
- You have now separated the date and time values into two separate columns. You can perform further calculations or analysis on them as needed.

If your date and time values are formatted differently, you may need to adjust the formulas accordingly. Also, make sure that the date and time values are in a consistent format before using these formulas.

Separate names in Excel – (First & Last Name)

Sometimes, you may have a column of names that are all listed together in a single cell, with the first and last names combined. This can make it difficult to sort or filter your data based on first or last name. The good news is that you can easily separate the first and last names into two separate columns using a few Excel formulas.

Step-by-Step Guide:

- Open your Excel workbook and navigate to the sheet containing the list of names.
- Insert two blank columns next to the column containing the combined names. These columns will be used to hold the first and last names.
- In the first blank column next to the combined names, enter the following formula in the first cell (assuming the first name is listed before the last name): =LEFT(A2,FIND(" ",A2)-1)
- This formula uses the LEFT function to extract the characters from the beginning of the cell up to the first space (which is assumed to separate the first and last names).
- Copy the formula down the entire column to apply it to all rows of data.
- In the second blank column next to the combined names, enter the following formula in the first cell: =RIGHT(A2,LEN(A2)-FIND(" ",A2))
- This formula uses the RIGHT function to extract the characters from the first space to the end of the cell (which is assumed to represent the last name).
- Copy the formula down the entire column to apply it to all rows of data.

- You can now hide or delete the original column containing the combined names if you no longer need it.

If the first and last names are not separated by a space, you can modify the formulas to use a different delimiter, such as a comma or hyphen.

Shortcut for Unhide Columns (Excel Shortcut)

When working with Excel, it's common to hide columns to declutter your worksheet. However, sometimes you may need to unhide a hidden column to view or edit its contents. Using the mouse to unhide columns can be time-consuming, especially if you have many hidden columns. Fortunately, there's a simple keyboard shortcut in Excel that can help you unhide columns quickly and easily.

Step-by-Step Guide:

- Open the Excel worksheet that contains the hidden columns you want to unhide.
- Select the column(s) to the left and right of the hidden column(s). Make sure you select the entire columns and not just a cell within them.
- Press and hold the "Ctrl" key on your keyboard and then press the "Shift" key.
- While still holding both keys, press the "0" (zero) key on your keyboard. This will unhide any columns that are hidden between the selected columns.
- Release all keys.

If you have multiple hidden columns that are not next to each other, you can repeat the above steps for each set of adjacent columns until all hidden columns are unhidden.

Show Formulas (Excel Shortcut)

In Excel, you can enter formulas to perform calculations and manipulate data. Sometimes, it may be necessary to view the formulas in a worksheet rather than the results they produce. The Show Formulas feature in Excel allows you to display all the formulas in your worksheet, making it easier to review and troubleshoot them.

Step-by-Step Guide:

- Open the Excel workbook you want to work with.
- Press the "Ctrl" key on your keyboard.
- While holding the "Ctrl" key, press the "`" key (the grave accent key) once. This will display all the formulas in your worksheet.
- If you want to switch back to displaying the results of the formulas, simply press "Ctrl + `" again.

The location of the "`" key may vary depending on your keyboard layout. It is usually located on the same key as the tilde (~) character.

Show Ruler in Excel

The ruler in Excel is a helpful tool that allows you to see the exact measurements of rows, columns, and margins on your worksheet. It can be particularly useful when you need to align objects or text boxes precisely.

Step-by-Step Guide:

- Open your Excel worksheet.
- Click on the "View" tab in the ribbon at the top of the screen.
- Look for the "Show" section on the ribbon and click the checkbox next to "Ruler."
- The ruler will now appear at the top and left-hand side of your worksheet.
- If you want to hide the ruler again, simply go back to the "View" tab and uncheck the "Ruler" box.

Smooth Line

In Excel, a smooth line is a line graph that connects data points with a smooth curve rather than a straight line. This can be useful for visualizing trends and patterns in your data that may not be as apparent with a traditional line graph.

Step-by-Step Guide:

- Enter your data into a worksheet and select the data range.
- Click on the "Insert" tab in the top menu bar.
- In the "Charts" section, click on the "Line" chart type dropdown and select "Line with Smoothed Lines."
- Excel will create a new chart with your data plotted as a smooth line.
- You can customize your chart by adding labels, titles, and adjusting the formatting as desired.
- To edit the chart at any time, simply click on the chart to activate it and use the "Chart Tools" menu that appears in the top menu bar.

The option for a smooth line may not be available in older versions of Excel, in which case you may need to manually create a smoothed line graph using a curve fitting technique.

Sort a Pivot Table in Excel

Pivot tables are a powerful tool in Excel that allow you to quickly summarize and analyze large amounts of data. However, it is important to be able to sort the data within a pivot table to make it easier to read and analyze.

Step-by-Step Guide:

- First, select any cell within the pivot table that you want to sort.
- On the Ribbon, click on the "Data" tab.
- In the "Sort & Filter" group, click on the "Sort Largest to Smallest" or "Sort Smallest to Largest" button to sort the data based on the selected column. Alternatively, click on the "Sort A to Z" or "Sort Z to A" button to sort the data based on the row labels.
- If you want to sort by multiple columns, click on the "Sort" button and select "More Sort Options". In the Sort dialog box, choose the columns to sort by and the sort order for each column.
- Click "OK" to apply the sorting to the pivot table.

The sorting options may vary depending on the version of Excel you are using.

Sort Buttons

Sorting data is a common task in Excel, and the software provides several tools to sort data in various ways. One of the most convenient ways to sort data is by using the sort buttons, which are located in the ribbon and provide quick access to frequently used sorting options. These buttons allow you to sort data in ascending or descending order based on one or more columns.

Step-by-Step Guide:

- Open your Excel worksheet with the data you want to sort.
- Select the column you want to sort by clicking on the column header.
- Click on the "Sort & Filter" button located in the "Home" tab of the ribbon.
- Select "Sort Smallest to Largest" or "Sort Largest to Smallest" depending on your preference.
- If you want to sort by more than one column, click on "Add Level" and select the next column you want to sort by.
- Repeat step 4 for each additional column you want to sort by.
- Click "OK" to apply the sorting to your data.
- Your data should now be sorted according to the criteria you selected.

The sort buttons can also be used to sort tables and pivot tables in a similar way. The options available in the "Sort & Filter" button may vary depending on the type of data you are working with.

Sort By Date, Date, and Time & Reverse Date Sort in Excel

Sorting data in Excel is a very useful and common task. Sorting by date or time can be particularly helpful when working with large datasets that include time-sensitive information. Excel offers a variety of sorting options, including sorting by date, time, or both. In this guide, we will cover how to sort data by date, time, and reverse date order in Excel.

Step-by-Step Guide:

- Select the range of cells that contains the data you want to sort.
- Click on the "Data" tab in the ribbon at the top of the screen.
- Click on the "Sort" button in the "Sort & Filter" section.
- In the "Sort" dialog box, select the column that contains the date data you want to sort by.
- In the "Sort On" dropdown menu, select "Values."
- In the "Order" dropdown menu, select "Oldest to Newest" or "Newest to Oldest" depending on how you want the data sorted.
- Click "OK" to sort the data.

How to Sort By Time in Excel:

- Select the range of cells that contains the data you want to sort.
- Click on the "Data" tab in the ribbon at the top of the screen.
- Click on the "Sort" button in the "Sort & Filter" section.

- In the "Sort" dialog box, select the column that contains the time data you want to sort by.
- In the "Sort On" dropdown menu, select "Values."
- In the "Order" dropdown menu, select "Oldest to Newest" or "Newest to Oldest" depending on how you want the data sorted.
- Click "OK" to sort the data.

How to Sort By Date and Time in Excel:

- Select the range of cells that contains the data you want to sort.
- Click on the "Data" tab in the ribbon at the top of the screen.
- Click on the "Sort" button in the "Sort & Filter" section.
- In the "Sort" dialog box, select the column that contains the date and time data you want to sort by.
- In the "Sort On" dropdown menu, select "Values."
- In the "Order" dropdown menu, select "Oldest to Newest" or "Newest to Oldest" depending on how you want the data sorted.
- Click "OK" to sort the data.

How to Sort By Reverse Date Order in Excel:

- Select the range of cells that contains the data you want to sort.
- Click on the "Data" tab in the ribbon at the top of the screen.
- Click on the "Sort" button in the "Sort & Filter" section.
- In the "Sort" dialog box, select the column that contains the date data you want to sort by.

- In the "Sort On" dropdown menu, select "Values."
- In the "Order" dropdown menu, select "Custom List."
- In the "List Entries" field, enter "1" and "2" to create a custom list.
- In the "Order" dropdown menu, select "Reverse Order."
- Click "OK" to sort the data in reverse date order.

You can also sort data by date, time, or reverse date order using the "Sort & Filter" dropdown menu on the Home tab.

SPEEDOMETER Chart in Excel

A speedometer chart is a graphical representation of data that resembles a car speedometer. It is useful for showing progress towards a goal or target, as well as for displaying performance metrics. In Excel, a speedometer chart can be created using a combination of a pie chart and a doughnut chart.

Step-by-Step Guide:

- Enter the data you want to represent in the speedometer chart into an Excel worksheet. The data should be in a single row or column.
- Select the data and click on the "Insert" tab in the Excel ribbon.
- Click on the "Pie" chart icon in the "Charts" section of the ribbon.
- Select the "Pie" chart type and choose the 2D option.
- Once the chart is created, right-click on the chart and choose "Select Data" from the context menu.
- Click on the "Add" button in the "Select Data Source" dialog box.
- In the "Edit Series" dialog box, enter a name for the series in the "Series Name" field.
- In the "Series Values" field, enter the cell reference for the data you want to represent in the speedometer chart.
- Click "OK" to close the "Edit Series" dialog box and return to the "Select Data Source" dialog box.
- In the "Select Data Source" dialog box, click on the "Edit" button next to the "Horizontal (Category) Axis Labels" field.
- In the "Axis Labels" dialog box, select the range of cells that contains the data labels for the chart.

- Click "OK" to close the "Axis Labels" dialog box and return to the "Select Data Source" dialog box.
- Click "OK" to close the "Select Data Source" dialog box and return to the chart.
- Right-click on the chart and choose "Change Chart Type" from the context menu.
- In the "Change Chart Type" dialog box, select the "Doughnut" chart type and choose the 2D option.
- Click "OK" to close the "Change Chart Type" dialog box and return to the chart.
- Right-click on the chart and choose "Select Data" from the context menu.
- In the "Select Data Source" dialog box, click on the "Add" button.
- In the "Edit Series" dialog box, enter a name for the series in the "Series Name" field.
- In the "Series Values" field, enter a formula that calculates the remaining value to be represented in the speedometer chart. The formula should be "=MAXVALUE-cell reference", where MAXVALUE is the maximum value for the data and cell reference is the cell containing the current value for the data.
- Click "OK" to close the "Edit Series" dialog box and return to the "Select Data Source" dialog box.
- Click "OK" to close the "Select Data Source" dialog box and return to the chart.
- Right-click on the chart and choose "Format Data Series" from the context menu.
- In the "Format Data Series" dialog box, choose "No Fill" for the "Fill" option and "No Line" for the "Border Color" option.
- Click "Close" to close the "Format Data Series" dialog box.
- Adjust the chart size and formatting as desired.

Spell Check in Excel

Excel is a powerful tool for analyzing and presenting data. When working with large amounts of data, it's important to ensure that everything is accurate and error-free. That's where the spell check feature in Excel comes in handy. Spell check can help you identify and correct spelling mistakes in your data, which can save you time and ensure that your data is accurate.

Step-by-Step Guide:

- Open the Excel file that you want to spell check.
- Click on the "Review" tab in the ribbon at the top of the screen.
- Click on the "Spelling" button in the ribbon. This will open the "Spelling" dialog box.
- The first spelling error will be highlighted in the dialog box. The suggested correction for the error will be displayed in the "Suggestions" box.
- If the suggested correction is correct, click the "Change" button to correct the error. If the suggested correction is not correct, select a different correction from the "Suggestions" box or manually correct the error in the "Not in Dictionary" box, and then click the "Change" button.
- Repeat the process for each spelling error in the dialog box until all errors have been corrected.
- If you want to ignore a spelling error, click the "Ignore" button. Excel will move on to the next spelling error.
- If you want to ignore all instances of a particular word, click the "Ignore All" button.
- If you want to add a word to the dictionary, type the word in the "Not in Dictionary" box and click the "Add" button.

- Once you have corrected all spelling errors, click the "OK" button to close the "Spelling" dialog box.

Square a Number in Excel

Excel is a powerful tool that can perform complex mathematical operations with ease. One such operation is to find the square of a number. Squaring a number means multiplying the number by itself. In Excel, there is a simple formula that can be used to calculate the square of a number.

Step-by-Step Guide:

- Open a new or existing Excel workbook.
- Enter the number that you want to square into a cell.
- Click on an empty cell where you want to display the result of the squared number.
- Type the equal sign (=) in the cell where you want to display the result.
- Type the cell reference of the cell containing the number you want to square, followed by the multiplication sign () and the same cell reference again. For example, if the number you want to square is in cell A1, then the formula would be "=A1A1".
- Press Enter to calculate the squared number.
- The result will appear in the cell where you typed the formula.

Status Bar

The status bar is located at the bottom of the Excel window and provides various useful information about the spreadsheet, such as the current cell selection, calculation mode, and average, minimum, and maximum values of selected cells.

Step-by-Step Guide:

- Open an Excel worksheet.
- Select any cell or range of cells to view the current selection on the status bar.
- Click on the "View" tab on the ribbon at the top of the Excel window.
- In the "Show" section, check the box next to "Status Bar" to enable it if it is not already enabled.
- Move your cursor to a cell with numerical data to see the sum, average, minimum, and maximum values displayed on the status bar.
- Highlight multiple cells to see the same statistics for the selected cells.
- Right-click on the status bar to customize the statistics displayed. You can choose to display other information like count, numerical count, and more.
- To turn off the status bar, simply uncheck the "Status Bar" option in the "Show" section of the "View" tab.

The status bar can also display other information, such as the progress of a task or the status of the Caps Lock and Num Lock keys.

Strikethrough

In Excel, strikethrough is a formatting option that allows you to apply a horizontal line through the center of a cell's contents. It is useful for indicating that certain information is no longer relevant or has been deleted while keeping it visible for reference purposes.

Step-by-Step Guide:

- Open the Excel spreadsheet that contains the cell or cells you want to format with strikethrough.
- Select the cell or cells you want to format.
- Click on the "Home" tab in the Excel ribbon.
- Look for the "Font" group on the Home tab.
- Click on the small down arrow icon next to the "Font Color" button.
- From the drop-down menu, select "Strikethrough" to apply the strikethrough formatting to the selected cell(s).
- You can also use a keyboard shortcut to apply strikethrough formatting to a cell or cells. Press and hold the "Ctrl" key on your keyboard and then press the "5" key. This will apply strikethrough formatting to the selected cell(s).
- To remove strikethrough formatting, repeat the steps above and select "Strikethrough" again to uncheck it.

Subscript (Excel Shortcut)

Subscript is a text formatting option in Excel that allows you to type text or numbers in a smaller font size and lower position than the rest of the text. It is often used in scientific and mathematical formulas to denote the base or index of a number. The subscript option in Excel can be accessed through a keyboard shortcut.

Step-by-Step Guide:

- Open an Excel worksheet and select the cell(s) where you want to add subscript.
- Type the text or number that you want to format as subscript.
- Place the cursor at the position where you want to start the subscript.
- Press the keyboard shortcut "Ctrl + =" (press and hold the Ctrl key, then press the equals sign).
- Type the text or number that you want to appear as the subscript.
- Press "Enter" to complete the entry.
- You can also access the subscript option through the "Font" section of the "Home" tab in the Excel ribbon. Select the text you want to format as subscript, then click on the "Subscript" button (X_2) in the "Font" section.

Sum an Entire Column or a Row in Excel

When working with large sets of data in Excel, it can be time-consuming to manually calculate the sum of an entire column or row. Fortunately, Excel provides a quick and easy way to sum up all the cells in a column or row using the SUM function. In this guide, we will show you how to use the SUM function to sum up an entire column or row in Excel.

Step-by-Step Guide:

- Open the Excel file containing the data you want to sum up.
- Select the cell where you want to display the total sum.
- Type the following formula in the selected cell: =SUM(column/row)
- Replace "column/row" with the letter of the column or number of the row you want to sum up. For example, if you want to sum up all the cells in column A, the formula would be =SUM(A:A). If you want to sum up all the cells in row 1, the formula would be =SUM(1:1).
- Press Enter to calculate the sum.
- The result of the sum will appear in the selected cell.

You can also use the AutoSum function to quickly sum up a column or row:

- Click on the cell immediately below the column you want to sum up or immediately to the right of the row you want to sum up.
- Click on the AutoSum button (Σ) in the Home tab of the Ribbon.

- Press Enter to calculate the sum.
- The result of the sum will appear in the selected cell.

Sum Greater Than Values using SUMIF

SUMIF is a powerful function in Excel that allows you to sum values based on a specific criteria. With the SUMIF function, you can easily sum values that are greater than a certain number.

Step-by-Step Guide:

- Open the Excel worksheet that contains the data you want to sum.
- Select a blank cell where you want to display the sum.
- Type the SUMIF formula in the selected cell. The syntax of the SUMIF formula is: =SUMIF(range, criteria, sum_range) where range is the range of cells that you want to evaluate, criteria is the criteria used to determine which cells to add, and sum_range is the range of cells that you want to sum.
- In the range argument, select the range of cells that you want to evaluate. For example, if you want to sum values in column B, select the range B:B.
- In the criteria argument, enter the criteria you want to use to determine which cells to add. To sum values that are greater than a certain number, use the "greater than" operator (>), followed by the number you want to use as the threshold. For example, to sum values greater than 100, enter ">100" in the criteria argument.
- In the sum_range argument, select the range of cells that you want to sum. For example, if you want to sum values in column C, select the range C:C.
- Press Enter to display the sum.

- The selected cell should now display the sum of the values that meet the criteria you specified.
- To verify that the function is working correctly, change the values in the range and observe how the sum changes accordingly.

Sum Not Equal Values (SUMIFS) in Excel

SUMIFS is a powerful function in Excel that allows you to sum values that meet multiple criteria. One such criteria is to sum only those values that are not equal to a certain value. This can be useful in scenarios where you want to exclude specific values from the sum calculation. In this guide, we will walk through the steps to sum not equal values using the SUMIFS function in Excel.

Step-by-Step Guide:

- Open Microsoft Excel and open the workbook that contains the data you want to sum.
- Select the cell where you want to display the sum result.
- Type the equal sign (=) to begin the formula.
- Type SUMIFS, followed by an opening parenthesis.
- Select the range of cells you want to sum, followed by a comma.
- Select the range of cells that contains the criteria to be evaluated, followed by a comma.
- Type the criteria you want to use for the evaluation. For example, to sum all values not equal to 100, you would type "<>100".
- Close the parenthesis and press enter to display the sum result.

You can add additional criteria by adding additional range/criteria pairs separated by commas in the SUMIFS formula. Also, make sure to use the correct syntax for the criteria based on the data type of the cells being evaluated. For example, text criteria should be enclosed in double quotes ("").

Sum Only Visible Cells in Excel

When you filter data in Excel, the hidden rows and columns are not included in the calculation of formulas such as SUM. If you want to sum only the visible cells in a filtered range, you can use the SUM function in combination with the SUBTOTAL function.

Step-by-Step Guide:

- Open your Excel spreadsheet and select the cell where you want to display the sum of visible cells.
- Type the equal sign "=" to start the formula.
- Type the function name "SUBTOTAL" followed by an opening parenthesis "(".
- Type "9" (the code for the SUM function) followed by a comma ",".
- Select the range of cells that you want to sum, making sure to include the header row if you have one.
- Close the parenthesis ")" for the range selection.
- Press "Enter" to complete the formula.
- Now apply a filter to your data range by selecting any cell in the data range and pressing "Ctrl+Shift+L" or going to the "Data" tab and clicking on "Filter".
- Filter the data range to hide some rows or columns.
- The cell where you entered the formula will now display the sum of only the visible cells in the filtered range.

If you add or remove rows or columns in your filtered range, the sum of visible cells will automatically adjust.

Sum Random Cells in Excel

The Sum Random Cells trick in Excel allows you to sum a random set of cells in a range. This is useful when you need to quickly calculate the total of a few random cells in a large data set.

Step-by-Step Guide:

- Open the Excel file and select the cell where you want to display the sum of the random cells.
- Type the formula =SUM(RAND()*[range]), replacing [range] with the actual range of cells you want to sum.
- Press Enter to calculate the sum. The result will be a random selection of cells within the specified range.
- If the result is not the desired set of cells, press F9 to recalculate the formula and generate a new set of random cells.
- If you want to sum a different set of random cells within the same range, simply press F9 to recalculate the formula and generate a new set of random cells.

This trick uses a random number generator to select the cells to be summed. Therefore, each time the formula is calculated, a new set of random cells will be selected. It is important to verify that the selected cells are the desired ones before using the result in any calculations or analysis.

SUMIF / SUMIFS with an OR Logic in Excel

SUMIF and SUMIFS are powerful functions in Excel that allow you to quickly sum values based on specific criteria. However, by default, these functions use AND logic, meaning that all the conditions must be met for the sum to be calculated. In some cases, you may want to use OR logic, where the sum is calculated if any of the conditions are met. In this case, you can use an array formula with the SUM function.

Step-by-Step Guide:

- Determine the criteria for the SUMIF/SUMIFS function. For example, you may want to sum values in column A if they are equal to "apples" OR "oranges."
- Set up an array with the criteria. In this example, you would enter {"apples","oranges"} into cells B1 and B2.
- In an adjacent cell, enter the following formula: =SUM((A1:A10=B1)+(A1:A10=B2)*A1:A10)
- Press Ctrl+Shift+Enter to enter the formula as an array formula. The formula will now appear with curly braces {} around it, indicating that it is an array formula.
- The result of the formula will be the sum of all values in column A that meet either of the criteria in the array.

If you are using SUMIFS instead of SUMIF, you will need to add additional criteria ranges and criteria to the formula. For example, if you also want to sum values in column B if they are greater than 5, you would add "+(B1:B10>5)" to the formula before the "*A1:A10" part.

SUMIF with Wildcard Characters in Excel

The SUMIF function in Excel is used to sum the values in a range of cells that meet a certain criteria. Wildcard characters are special characters used to represent one or more characters when searching for a specific pattern in a text string. Using wildcard characters in the criteria of the SUMIF function allows you to sum values based on a partial match or a pattern match.

Step-by-Step Guide:

- Open a new or existing Excel spreadsheet.
- Enter the data that you want to work with in the spreadsheet. For example, you might have a list of sales amounts for different products.
- Decide on the criteria that you want to use for summing the values. For example, you might want to sum the sales amounts for all products that contain the word "apple".
- Type "=SUMIF(" into the cell where you want the result to appear. This will activate the SUMIF function.
- Enter the range of cells that you want to search for the criteria. For example, if your data is in cells A1 to A10, you would enter "A1:A10".
- Enter the criteria that you want to use for the sum. For example, if you want to sum the sales amounts for all products that contain the word "apple", you would enter "apple" as the criteria. The asterisk (*) is the wildcard character that represents any number of characters.
- Enter the range of cells that you want to sum. For example, if your sales amounts are in cells B1 to B10, you would enter "B1:B10".

- Close the parentheses and press Enter. The sum of the sales amounts that meet the criteria will appear in the cell.

SUMIFS Date Range (Sum Values Between Two Dates Array)

The SUMIFS function in Excel allows you to sum values that meet multiple criteria. One common use case is to sum values within a date range. This can be useful for financial or project management purposes, where you want to track expenses or progress within a certain time frame.

Step-by-Step Guide:

- Create a new Excel spreadsheet or open an existing one where you want to sum values between two dates.
- Enter your data in the spreadsheet. Be sure to include a column with dates and another column with values that you want to sum. For example, you could have a column with dates in column A and a column with corresponding expenses in column B.
- Decide on the date range you want to sum. For example, you might want to sum expenses between January 1st and January 31st.
- In an empty cell where you want to display the sum, type the following formula:
  =SUMIFS(B:B, A:A, ">="&DATE(year, month, day), A:A, "<="&DATE(year, month, day))
- Replace "B:B" with the column containing the values you want to sum (in our example, column B). Replace "A:A" with the column containing the dates (in our example, column A). Replace "year", "month", and "day" with the start date of your range (in our example, 2023, 01, 01 for January 1st) and the end date of your range (in our example, 2023, 01, 31 for January 31st).
- Press enter to display the sum.

SUMPRODUCT IF

SUMPRODUCT is a powerful function in Excel that can perform calculations on multiple arrays of data. One of the advanced features of the SUMPRODUCT function is the ability to use it with IF statements, which allows you to selectively sum values based on specific criteria. This trick is called SUMPRODUCT IF.

Step-by-Step Guide:

- Begin by opening an Excel workbook and navigating to a blank worksheet.
- Enter the data you want to work with in the worksheet. This data can be in any format, but it should contain at least one column of values you want to sum based on specific criteria.
- Define the criteria you want to use for the SUMPRODUCT IF calculation. This can be done by creating a separate range of cells that contain the criteria you want to use. For example, if you want to sum values that are greater than 10, you would create a cell with the value "10" in it.
- Enter the SUMPRODUCT function in a blank cell where you want to display the result of the calculation. The basic syntax of the SUMPRODUCT function is "=SUMPRODUCT(array1,array2,...)". You will need to enter the arrays you want to include in the calculation inside the parentheses. For example, if you want to sum the values in column B based on the criteria in cell A1, you would enter the formula "=SUMPRODUCT((B1:B10>A1)*B1:B10)".
- Press enter to complete the formula. The result of the SUMPRODUCT IF calculation will be displayed in the cell where you entered the formula.

SUMPRODUCT IF to Create a Conditional Formula in Excel

In Excel, the SUMPRODUCT IF function is a powerful tool that allows you to sum the products of corresponding arrays or ranges of cells, based on one or more specified conditions. With this function, you can perform complex calculations and filter data based on specific criteria, without the need for multiple formulas or steps.

Step-by-Step Guide:

- Open the Excel worksheet and select a cell where you want to display the result.
- Type the formula =SUMPRODUCT((range1=condition1)*(range2 =condition2)*range3) in the cell, where:
    o range1 and condition1 are the range and condition to check for the first criterion.
    o range2 and condition2 are the range and condition to check for the second criterion (if required).
    o range3 is the range of cells to multiply and sum.
- Press the Enter key to apply the formula and get the result.

The conditions should be written in double quotes if they are text strings or enclosed in quotation marks (e.g. ">10") if they are numeric or date values.

Superscript (Excel Shortcut)

In Excel, superscript is a formatting option that allows you to make selected text appear slightly above the normal text line. This is useful for displaying exponents, footnotes, or any other text that needs to be raised above the normal text line.

Step-by-Step Guide:

- Select the text that you want to format as superscript.
- Use the following keyboard shortcut: "Ctrl" + "Shift" + "+". This will apply superscript formatting to the selected text.
- To remove superscript formatting, select the superscript text and use the following keyboard shortcut: "Ctrl" + "Shift" + "-". This will remove the superscript formatting and return the text to normal formatting.

Switch Tabs (Excel Shortcut)

Switching between tabs in Excel can be time-consuming, especially when you have a lot of worksheets open. Using the "Switch Tabs" Excel shortcut can save you time and make your work more efficient.

Step-by-Step Guide:

- Open Microsoft Excel and open multiple worksheets.
- Look at the bottom left corner of the Excel window, where you will see a list of tabs representing each open worksheet.
- To switch to the next worksheet, press and hold the "Ctrl" key on your keyboard and then press the "Tab" key. You will see the active worksheet switch to the next one in the list.
- To switch to the previous worksheet, press and hold the "Ctrl" key on your keyboard and then press the "Shift" and "Tab" keys at the same time. You will see the active worksheet switch to the previous one in the list.

You can use this shortcut to quickly navigate through your worksheets and find the one you need.

Theme Color

Excel allows users to format cells, charts, and other objects with various color schemes. Theme colors are a set of 12 colors that can be customized according to the user's preference. These colors can be used to create a consistent look and feel throughout a workbook, making it easier to read and understand.

Step-by-Step Guide:

- Open Excel and create a new workbook or open an existing one.
- Click on the "Page Layout" tab on the ribbon at the top of the screen.
- Look for the "Themes" section on the ribbon.
- Click on the drop-down menu under "Themes" to see the available theme options.
- Hover your mouse over a theme to see a preview of how it will look in your workbook.
- Click on a theme to apply it to your workbook.
- To customize the colors in the theme, click on the "Colors" drop-down menu under the "Themes" section.
- Choose "Customize Colors" at the bottom of the drop-down menu.
- The "Create New Theme Colors" dialog box will appear.
- Choose a color to customize by clicking on it.
- Choose a new color from the color palette or enter the RGB color code.
- Repeat steps 10 and 11 for each of the 12 theme colors.
- When finished customizing, give your new theme a name and click "Save".

- Your new theme will now appear in the "Themes" drop-down menu for future use.

Theme colors can be applied to various objects in Excel such as charts, tables, and shapes. To apply a theme color to an object, select the object and click on the appropriate color in the "Themes" section of the ribbon.

Thermometer Chart in Excel

A thermometer chart is a visual representation of data that resembles a thermometer, used to show progress towards a goal. It can be used to represent the progress of a fundraising campaign, sales goals, or any other metrics that have a target value. The chart is created using a stacked column chart and formatting techniques in Excel.

Step-by-Step Guide:

- Enter your data : Enter your data into an Excel worksheet. You need two values: the current value and the target value. For example, let's say you are tracking a fundraising campaign and have raised $10,000 out of a target of $50,000.
- Create a stacked column chart : Select the data range you just entered and insert a stacked column chart from the "Insert" tab in the Excel ribbon.
- Format the chart : Right-click on the chart and select "Format Chart Area." In the Format Chart Area pane, choose a fill color for the chart, such as red to represent the temperature of the thermometer.
- Add a data label : Right-click on the chart and select "Add Data Labels." The data labels will appear above each section of the chart.
- Format the data label : Select the data label and right-click to format it. In the Format Data Labels pane, choose "Value From Cells" and select the cell containing the current value. This will replace the data label with the value from the cell.
- Adjust the axis : Right-click on the axis and select "Format Axis." In the Format Axis pane, set the minimum value to 0, the maximum value to the target value, and the major unit to the target value

divided by 10. This will adjust the axis to match the target value.
- Adjust the data series : Click on one of the data series in the chart and adjust the gap width to 0% in the "Format Data Series" pane. This will remove the gap between the sections of the chart, giving the appearance of a solid thermometer.
- Add the target line : Right-click on the chart and select "Add Chart Element" > "Lines" > "Target Value." In the "Format Horizontal Line" pane, set the value to the target value and format the line style and color to your preference. This will add a horizontal line to the chart at the target value.
- Add a title : Add a title to the chart by clicking on the chart and entering the text in the "Chart Title" field in the Excel ribbon.

Transpose (Excel Shortcut)

Transpose is a useful feature in Excel that allows you to switch the orientation of data in a range of cells. Instead of having data arranged in rows, it allows you to rearrange it in columns and vice versa. This can be especially useful when you want to perform calculations or analysis on a different set of data.

Step-by-Step Guide:

- Open an Excel workbook and enter the data you want to transpose in a range of cells.
- Select the range of cells you want to transpose.
- Right-click on the selected cells and choose "Copy" or use the "Ctrl + C" shortcut to copy the data.
- Right-click on the cell where you want to paste the transposed data.
- Click on the "Paste Special" option or press the "Ctrl + Alt + V" shortcut to open the "Paste Special" dialog box.
- In the "Paste Special" dialog box, check the "Transpose" box located at the bottom-left corner of the box.
- Click the "OK" button to transpose the data from rows to columns or vice versa.

You can also use the "Transpose" function to transpose data in Excel. The function syntax is "=TRANSPOSE(array)" where "array" is the range of cells you want to transpose.

Undo-Redo

Undo and Redo are two very useful commands in Excel that allow you to undo or redo the last actions you performed. This can be very helpful if you accidentally delete or change something in your spreadsheet that you didn't intend to. The Undo command can help you revert to the previous state of your spreadsheet, while the Redo command can help you go back to the changes you just undid.

Step-by-Step Guide:

- To use the Undo command, simply click on the "Undo" button located in the Quick Access Toolbar at the top of the Excel window. You can also use the keyboard shortcut "Ctrl + Z" to perform this action.
- To use the Redo command, click on the "Redo" button located next to the "Undo" button in the Quick Access Toolbar. You can also use the keyboard shortcut "Ctrl + Y" to perform this action.
- You can use the Undo and Redo commands multiple times in succession to undo or redo several changes in your spreadsheet.
- If you want to undo or redo a specific action that you performed, you can right-click on the cell or range of cells that was affected by the action, and then select "Undo" or "Redo" from the context menu.
- If you want to view a list of all the actions you have performed in your spreadsheet, click on the "File" tab in the Ribbon at the top of the Excel window, and then select "Info" from the left-hand menu. From there, click on the "Manage Workbook" button, and then select "Revisions" to

view a list of all the changes made to your spreadsheet.
- Finally, it's important to note that the Undo and Redo commands have limits. You can only undo or redo up to the last 100 actions performed in your spreadsheet. If you need to go further back in time, you'll need to use Excel's version history feature, which allows you to view and restore earlier versions of your spreadsheet.

View Two Sheets Side by Side in Excel

Viewing two sheets side by side in Excel is a useful feature that allows users to compare and analyze data from two different worksheets at the same time. This feature can be especially helpful for users who need to compare data or formulas from different sheets, or who want to monitor changes made to one sheet while working on another.

Step-by-Step Guide:

- Open the Excel workbook that contains the two sheets you want to view side by side.
- Click on the "View" tab in the Excel ribbon at the top of the screen.
- In the "Window" group, click on the "View Side by Side" button. This will open a new window with the two sheets side by side.
- If Excel does not automatically arrange the windows side by side, you can manually adjust the window size and position by clicking and dragging the borders of each window.
- To turn off the "View Side by Side" feature, simply click on the "View Side by Side" button again.

You can also use the keyboard shortcut "Alt + W, S" to quickly toggle the "View Side by Side" feature on and off.

VLOOKUP MATCH Combination in Excel

VLOOKUP is a popular function in Excel used to look up and retrieve data from a specific column in a table. However, it only looks for exact matches, which can be limiting. MATCH is another function that can be used to locate a value in a table, but it doesn't retrieve any data. By combining VLOOKUP and MATCH, we can overcome the limitations of VLOOKUP and retrieve data based on partial matches. This trick is called the VLOOKUP MATCH combination.

Step-by-Step Guide:

- Start by opening a new or existing Excel file containing the data you want to work with.
- Identify the table you want to work with. This table should contain the data you want to retrieve using the VLOOKUP MATCH combination.
- Determine the column number of the data you want to retrieve. This is the column that contains the data you want to retrieve based on partial matches.
- Create a separate table or list where you want to display the retrieved data.
- In the first cell of the table where you want to display the retrieved data, enter the VLOOKUP formula: =VLOOKUP(lookup_value, table_array, MATCH(lookup_value, lookup_array, 0), [range_lookup])
- Replace "lookup_value" in the formula with the cell reference of the value you want to search for.
- Replace "table_array" in the formula with the range of cells that contains the table you want to search in. Make sure that the left-most column in this range is the column where the lookup values are located.

- Replace "lookup_array" in the formula with the range of cells that contains the lookup values. This range should only include the column where the lookup values are located.
- Replace "range_lookup" in the formula with "FALSE" if you want to find an exact match or "TRUE" if you want to find an approximate match. Using "FALSE" ensures that the lookup function only returns exact matches.
- Press Enter to complete the formula.
- The first cell in the table should now display the retrieved data based on the partial match.
- Copy the formula to the rest of the cells in the table to retrieve the data for all lookup values.

VLOOKUP with Multiple Criteria in Excel

VLOOKUP is a powerful function in Excel that allows you to search for a specific value in a table and return a related value. However, it can only search for one specific criteria. If you need to search for multiple criteria, you can use a combination of functions to achieve this, including VLOOKUP and IF.

Step-by-Step Guide:

- First, make sure your data is organized in a table. This means that each column should have a header and each row should represent a unique record.
- Identify the criteria you need to search for. Let's say you want to search for a product in a table based on its name and category.
- Create a helper column that combines the two criteria into one cell. For example, you can create a new column and use the "&" operator to combine the name and category columns. This will create a unique identifier for each record.
- Use the VLOOKUP function to search for the value in the new helper column. The formula should include the lookup value, the table range, the column index number, and the exact match parameter. For example, if your helper column is in column E, your formula might look like this:
- =VLOOKUP(G2,$A$2:$E$10,5,0)
- The result of the VLOOKUP formula will be the related value in the same row as the matched record. However, if there are multiple records that match the criteria, the formula will only return the first match.
- To account for multiple matches, you can use the IF function to create a nested formula. This will

allow you to search for multiple matches and return a specific result for each one. For example, you can use the following formula to search for all matches and return a comma-separated list of related values:
- =IF($E$2:$E$10=G2,$D$2:$D$10&", ","")
- The result of the IF formula will be a list of values that match the criteria. You can then use a separate formula, such as CONCATENATE, to combine the values into a single cell if needed.

Wildcard Characters in Excel

In Excel, wildcard characters are special characters used to represent one or more characters in a text string. Using wildcard characters can help you search for and manipulate data more efficiently and effectively.

Step-by-Step Guide:

- Asterisk (*) - represents any number of characters:
  The asterisk wildcard character represents any number of characters in a text string. For example, if you want to search for all cells containing the word "apple" regardless of what comes before or after it, you can use the following formula in the Find and Replace dialog box: "apple".
- Question mark (?) - represents a single character:
  The question mark wildcard character represents a single character in a text string. For example, if you want to search for all cells containing a four-letter word that starts with "s" and ends with "t", you can use the following formula in the Find and Replace dialog box: "s??t".
- Tilde () - used to escape special characters:
  The tilde wildcard character is used to escape other wildcard characters and special characters in a text string. For example, if you want to search for all cells containing the asterisk character (*), you can use the following formula in the Find and Replace dialog box: "*".
- Bracket ([])- used to specify a range of characters:
  The bracket wildcard characters are used to specify a range of characters. For example, if you want to search for all cells containing a vowel, you can use the following formula in the Find and Replace dialog box: "[aeiou]".

- Bracket with hyphen (-) - used to specify a range of characters:
  The bracket wildcard characters with a hyphen are used to specify a range of characters. For example, if you want to search for all cells containing a letter between "a" and "d", you can use the following formula in the Find and Replace dialog box: "[a-d]".

Wildcards with VLOOKUP in Excel

VLOOKUP function in Excel is used to search for a value in the first column of a table and then return a corresponding value from the same row in another column of the table. Wildcard characters can be used with VLOOKUP to match values that contain specific characters, patterns or combinations of characters.

Step-by-Step Guide:

- Start by opening a new or existing Excel file that contains data to be searched with VLOOKUP.
- Click on the cell where you want the result to be displayed.
- Type in the formula "=VLOOKUP(" in the formula bar.
- Enter the cell reference of the lookup value in the first argument of the VLOOKUP function, followed by a comma. For example, if you want to lookup a value in cell A2, you should type A2 after the equal sign and before the comma.
- Enter the table range in the second argument of the VLOOKUP function, followed by a comma. The table range should include the column that contains the lookup value and the column that contains the result to be returned. For example, if the table range is A1:B10, column A should contain the lookup values and column B should contain the results to be returned.
- Enter the column index number of the result to be returned in the third argument of the VLOOKUP function, followed by a comma. The column index number should be a positive integer that represents the column number of the table range that contains the result to be returned. For

example, if the result you want is in column B, you should enter "2".
- Add a final argument to the VLOOKUP function to include the wildcard characters. Wildcard characters can be added within the lookup value, the first argument of the VLOOKUP function. The following wildcard characters are available in Excel:
    o Asterisk (*) – Matches any sequence of characters.
    o Question mark (?) – Matches any single character.
    o For example, if you want to search for all values that start with "A", you should use the formula "=VLOOKUP("A*", A1:B10, 2, FALSE)".
- Press "Enter" to complete the formula and display the result.

Worksheet Copy

Copying a worksheet in Excel allows you to create a duplicate of an existing worksheet. This can be useful in situations where you want to create multiple versions of the same worksheet or you want to make changes to the original worksheet while preserving a copy of the original. In this guide, we will walk you through the steps for copying a worksheet in Excel.

Step-by-Step Guide:

- Open the Excel workbook that contains the worksheet you want to copy.
- Right-click on the worksheet tab that you want to copy.
- From the right-click menu, select "Move or Copy."
- In the "Move or Copy" dialog box, select the workbook where you want to copy the worksheet to.
- In the "Before sheet" section, choose where you want to place the copied worksheet.
- Check the "Create a copy" checkbox at the bottom of the dialog box.
- Click on the "OK" button to create a copy of the worksheet.

You can also use the keyboard shortcut "Ctrl + Drag" to copy a worksheet within the same workbook. Simply hold down the "Ctrl" key while dragging the worksheet tab to the location where you want to copy it. Release the mouse button and then the "Ctrl" key to complete the copy.

Write (Type) Vertically in Excel

Sometimes you may want to write text vertically in Excel instead of horizontally. This can be useful when creating headers or when you want to save space on your spreadsheet. The good news is that it's easy to write vertically in Excel using the text box feature.

Step-by-Step Guide:

- Click on the cell where you want to insert the vertical text.
- Go to the "Insert" tab on the ribbon and click on the "Text Box" button in the "Text" group.
- Click and drag on the worksheet to create a text box.
- Type the text that you want to appear vertically in the text box.
- With the text box selected, go to the "Format" tab on the ribbon.
- In the "Text Box Styles" group, click on the "Text Direction" button.
- Choose the vertical text direction that you want to use. You can choose from "Vertical" or "Rotate 90 degrees".
- Adjust the size and position of the text box as needed.
- If you want to remove the border of the text box, right-click on the text box and select "Format Text Box".
- In the "Format Text Box" dialog box, select "No line" under "Line Color".
- Click "Close" to close the dialog box.

Years Between Dates in Excel

In Excel, you can calculate the number of years between two dates using a simple formula. This can be useful for various purposes such as calculating the age of a person, calculating the number of years between two events, or calculating the length of a project in years.

Step-by-Step Guide:

- Open Excel and create a new worksheet.
- In cell A1, enter the start date of the period you want to calculate the number of years for. Make sure to format the cell as a date using the "Short Date" format.
- In cell B1, enter the end date of the period you want to calculate the number of years for. Again, format the cell as a date.
- In cell C1, enter the following formula: =YEAR(B1)-YEAR(A1)
- Press Enter to calculate the number of years between the two dates.
- Format cell C1 as a number to remove any decimal places.
- You should now see the number of years between the two dates in cell C1.

This formula calculates the number of years based on the difference in the year values between the two dates. It does not take into account any additional months or days beyond the year values. If you need a more precise calculation that takes into account the additional time periods, you can use the DATEDIF function in Excel.

Zoom-In (Excel Shortcut)

Excel provides various features to make data analysis and presentation easier for users. One of such features is the Zoom-In option which allows the user to zoom in on the selected area to have a better and detailed view of the data. This feature comes in handy especially when dealing with a large dataset or when the user wants to focus on specific data.

Step-by-Step Guide:

- Select the cell or the range of cells that you want to zoom in on.
- You can zoom in using the following methods:
    - Press and hold the Ctrl key on your keyboard, and scroll up the mouse wheel to zoom in.
    - Alternatively, click on the "View" tab on the top menu bar.
    - In the "Zoom" group, click on the "Zoom In" button to zoom in on the selected cell or range of cells.
- You can also use the Zoom slider located at the bottom right-hand corner of the Excel window. Simply click and drag the slider to the right to zoom in on the selected cell or range of cells.

To zoom out, you can use the following methods:

- Press and hold the Ctrl key on your keyboard, and scroll down the mouse wheel to zoom out.
- Alternatively, click on the "View" tab on the top menu bar.
- In the "Zoom" group, click on the "Zoom Out" button to zoom out on the selected cell or range of cells.

- You can also use the Zoom slider located at the bottom right-hand corner of the Excel window. Simply click and drag the slider to the left to zoom out on the selected cell or range of cells.

Printed in Great Britain
by Amazon